The Spirit of Texas

ACTIVITY GUIDE

A Unique Approach to Learning
Texas History

WRITTEN BY YVONNE CUMBERLAND AND LAURIE COCKERELL

Kinderfable Press
Fort Worth, Texas

Dedications

*To Charlie . . . who already loves books and I'm sure will patiently endure
many a Texas history story cuddled up on my lap.*
-Laurie Cockerell

*I would like to dedicate this book to the "men" in my life:
My grandpa, Cletus Batto, who first instilled in me a love for writing
with simple poems on a chalkboard behind the back door and who always, no matter what,
stopped and read every historical marker—even if we had read them the week before.
My daddy, Matthew Hutzler, who always made me feel special and find the positive in everything.
And to my three sons—Ben, Jeff and Luke, who accept me for who I am, encourage me and my crazy ideas,
don't roll their eyes when I run into someone I know every single time we go somewhere and now, just laugh
because if I don't run into someone I know, I've instead become friends with the waiter or sales clerk.
Love to you all, in heaven and on earth.   - Yvonne Cumberland*

Kinderfable Press
P.O. Box 10193
Fort Worth, Texas 76114
www.kinderfablepress.com

ISBN 978-0-9845609-4-3

Printed in the United States of America

A GUIDE TO
The Spirit of Texas History Curriculum

Texas history.

Those two words evoke either cheers and smiles of pride, or eyes rolled with boredom. Families and teachers with strong Texas roots often instill an unbreakable bond and love of the Lone Star State in their children. They know the remarkable stories of Texas. Stories of fascinating Native Americans, eighteen-minute battles that changed the world, and fallen heroes trapped inside the walls of an old mission, fighting for liberty or death.

Unfortunately, history is also sometimes viewed as dry mountains of memorization. Names and dates. Rules and laws.

The authors of this curriculum view Texas history as a portal to adventure. Both have spent many years teaching, speaking, and writing about this fascinating topic, encouraging children to not only accumulate knowledge, but to see Texas as they see it: an incredible source of ongoing fascination and excitement.

The Spirit of Texas curriculum offers a unique perspective on teaching Texas history. The *Daily Reading Book*, used in tandem with the companion *Activity Guide* and *Reproducible Book*, provides a total, cross-curricular experience for your family or classroom. History doesn't stop with just the presentation of facts; a multitude of additional exercises and games offered within the companion books will help build a foundation of knowledge and understanding beyond a simple reading of history. Extend your students' understanding of Texas facts and lore through math, writing, science, art, music, and other extension exercises. The curriculum is geared toward students between 4th and 7th grade, but can easily be adjusted for younger or older children.

Please note that there are three books included in this curriculum:
1. **DAILY READING BOOK:** This is the foundation of the curriculum: the history textbook.
2. **ACTIVITY GUIDE:** This book will lead your students through activities related to their reading of the day. Some activities are fully explained in the guide, while other directions will be found on the worksheets in the *Reproducible Book*. Copy work, recipes, and the answer key locations in the *Activity Guide* will be noted with the letters "AG" and page number location.
3. **REPRODUCIBLE BOOK:** Reproducible activities and unit tests assigned in the *Activity Guide* are noted by the letters "RB" and the page number location.

We suggest your student begin each unit by reading from the *Daily Reading Book* (as your schedule allows), followed by the activities suggested in the *Activity Guide* (choose according to time available and suitability to your students). You will find a suggested nine-month schedule on page 6, but this curriculum is designed to be flexible and meet your programming needs. Complete as much or as little as you prefer each day.

Texas history education doesn't end with the close of the book. Continue this fascinating journey of knowledge through visits to the many suggested museums and other landmarks listed at the end of each unit in the activity book. Select books from the *Suggested Reading* and make history come to life. Help your students understand that Texas is not just a place on a map or a list of facts and dates.

Teach them that THEY are Texas!

TABLE OF CONTENTS

DAILY READING UNITS

APPENDIX

September	*Texas Symbols and Regions*	*Westfest* West, Tx.
October	*Native Americans in Texas*	*"Come and Take It" Festival* Gonzales, Tx. *Texian Market Days* George Ranch Historical Park *Oktoberfest* Fredericksburg, Tx
November	*Explorers and Missionaries*	*Civil War Reenactment* Liendo, Tx. *Wurstfest* New Braunfels, Tx
December	*Filibusters and Empresarios*	*Dickens on the Strand* Galveston, Tx
January	*Revolution!*	*Fort Worth Stock Show and Rodeo* Fort Worth, Tx
February	*Finish Revolution/ Republic of Texas*	*Buffalo Soldier Heritage Day* San Angelo *Mardi Gras Festival* Galveston, Tx
March	*Statehood and Civil War*	*Texas Independence Day* Washington-on-the-Brazos *Goliad Massacre Reenactment and Living History*
April	*Cowboys & Indians/ Texas in the 20th Century*	*San Jacinto Day* La Porte, Texas *Folkfest* New Braunfels
May	*Finish 20th Century/ Texas Government*	*Sam Houston Folk Festival* Huntsville June: *Texas Folklife Festival* San Antonio July: *Ysleta Mission Festival* El Paso

Activity Guide

Although the majority of the activities included in this book are easily understood, please read directions and suggestions regarding these experiences to make the most of your Texas history curriculum. A suggested schedule for the school year can be found on page 6. Feel free to adjust time allotted, the activities, and the focus of instruction. If your students develop a strong interest in Sam Houston, for example, by all means take a break and let them dig deeper and become experts on Texas history and its heroes. Use the suggested readings, websites, movies, and more following each unit section to extend your students' studies on various topics.

IMPORTANT: *Be sure to make copies of your templates,*
so they can be used over and over again throughout the curriculum!!

We also recommend each student keep a three-ring binder to collect completed worksheets, copy work, and unit tests throughout the year. Use labeled dividers to separate work by units or activities.

Copy Work: Most students who use this curriculum will have already received instruction in cursive writing. We suggest these short copy work activities be completed in cursive, and students will also enjoy including a beautiful illustration to go along with the entry. Some of the entries are short and included in the *Activity Guide*, while others should be found with an online search. We have provided some links to websites which we realize may not remain active over time; however, these documents can be easily found with an additional web search using key words.

Vocabulary: We have provided a list of vocabulary words for sections within each unit (vocabulary words are bold and italicized within the reading lesson). Fill in the vocabulary windowpanes found in the *Reproducible Book* to define and illustrate each word; save completed windowpanes in the binder for occasional or year-end vocabulary review.

Timeline: Use the Timeline template located in the *Reproducible Book* to keep an ongoing chronological account of events occurring consecutively in Texas, the U.S., and the world while studying the curriculum. Cut on the dotted lines, add a date in the small oval, and note important events in each section for that year. Tape together as time progresses.

KWL Charts: Begin each unit by having students fill in the first and middle sections: first, what they already *know* about the unit topic (K), and then what they *want* to learn about the topic (W). After completing the unit, they will fill in the third section, noting facts they *learned* in their study of the unit (L).

Look It Up Questions: It's important that students learn to use both contemporary technology and the good old library to research facts and figures. A separate "Look It Up" section should be kept within the student's binder throughout the year. Students might even enjoy writing questions for other students to research!

What If? Questions: It is, of course, important for students to memorize and understand facts. But it's also essential for them to critically analyze the relevance of events and historical characters. One way to achieve that goal is to consider how our state, country, and world might be completely different if events had occurred in some other way. Talk about the domino effect and how the outcome of history can easily change with just one person's decision. Students can either orally discuss potential outcomes, or use the question as a writing prompt for a persuasive argument exercise.

Twenty Questions Game: Played for generations, this is the classic game of elimination. Copy the template and make a set of cards for each unit, using the suggested people/things or create your own ideas. One player picks a card, and the other players try to guess who/what the first player selected by asking only yes or no questions, narrowing down the possibilities using the process of elimination. Remember to start with general questions (for example: *Are you a person? A place? A thing?*). Save cards from each unit for future review. *Index cards also work well for this activity.*

Charades: Use the *Twenty Questions* cards to play charades. Pick a card and "act out" the word, using only hand and body gestures. Decide in advance if the number of words or syllables will be used as hints.

Memory Game: Use two identical sets of the completed *Twenty Questions* game cards. Turn all cards face-side down in random order. Flip two over at a time, trying to match two identical cards. If they don't match, flip both back over and try to remember where they are located. Continue play and keep the set of matching cards once they are finally turned over at the same time. When all cards are matched, the player with the most cards wins!

It's About Time! Game: Play this game to remember the order of important historic events. Using the template, cut out separate rectangular cards. At the end of most units, a list of dates and events are provided in the *It's About Time* section. On one side of each card, label and illustrate the event; on the reverse side, write the date of the event (make sure you can't see the date through the card). Deal an even number of cards to each player and place cards, illustration side up, on the table. First player lays a card, date side down, on the table. Next player chooses one of his/her cards and places it to the left if he/she believes the event occurred before, or to the right if it occurred after, the date of the first card. Turn over both cards to check for accuracy. Got it right? If not, move it to the correct position. If correct, the next player places a card in order and checks accuracy. First player out of cards wins. Keep cards from previous units to play longer and longer games (just make sure you have room on your table—you might have to play on the floor!).

Art To Explore: Sometimes we forget about using the beauty of art as a teaching tool. We've provided some examples of artwork which will hopefully inspire your students to a better understanding of Texas history and important Texas personalities. This artwork might provide a writing prompt or an inspiration to create a similar work in a different style . . . or perhaps a similar style with a different theme. We hope students will find an appreciation for this type of communication, and will perhaps discover new favorite artists or styles. Each suggested artwork is easily found online with a search using the piece's title and artist.

Music: Even if the students and teacher are not musicians, it's easy to find recordings of the songs listed online, especially as a YouTube video. It's fun to find these songs and sing along! Most are considered classics and are examples of some of the important musical pieces in our country and state's history.

Websites: While the links and websites suggested in this curriculum were active at the time of publication, we understand time marches on and links become inactive and websites don't live forever. If this occurs, you should be able to do an online search with important keywords to find the primary source or other resource mentioned.

Places to Visit: While the authors have toured many of the suggested sites, we have not visited all that are listed. Please be sure to check out their websites prior to your visit for current status, hours of operation, and exhibitions.

Books and Movies: The books listed include both non-fiction and historical fiction titles. While the majority of the selections are appropriate for elementary and up, a few books are noted to be for older children and adults. Most books should be available through your public/school library system and most certainly through Amazon or other online shopping sources.

Comic Strips: Your students will enjoy creating comic strips as they stroll through Texas history. Remind them to reduce stories to the most important scenes, using labels and speech bubbles if needed. Create a title for the comic strip in the frame provided at the top of the page.

Unit Tests: Unit tests should be completed at the close of each unit. An answer key is available for unit tests and other exercises in the *Activity Guide*.

Answer Keys: We have provided a list of answers to the Unit Tests, *Look It Ups,* and most of the other activities in the *Activity Guide* appendix.

SUGGESTED RESOURCES TO ENHANCE THIS CURRICULUM

Books (General Topics About Texas)
Texas History Timeline: From Indians to Astronauts by Betsy Warren. Dallas: Hendrick-Long, 1996.
Texas History Supplemental Text by Cindy Sandell. Plano: VIS Enterprises, 2004.
Texas Parks and Wildlife Magazine: https://www.tpwmagazine.com/
Texas: An Album of History by James Haley. Garden City: Doubleday, 1985. [teens/adults]
The Story of Texas by John Edward Weems. Fredericksburg: Shearer Publishing, 1986.
Texas History for Kids: Lone Star Lives and Legends by Karen Bush Gibson. Chicago: Chicago Review Press, 2015.
Ballads of Texas History by Fred Cooper. Frisco: Sing 'n Learn Publications, 2015.
We suggest you order or download travel brochures from the following:
https://www.tourtexas.com/travel-guides *and* http://www.thc.texas.gov/explore-texas

Movies
Texas History Documentaries: http://birthoftexas.com/spanish-texas.html
Sam Houston and Texas History: http://samhoustonmovie.com/index.php/samh/videos
Texas history documentaries, books, and resources: www.texashistory.com

Websites
Lone Star Junction: http://www.lsjunction.com/
Texas Beyond History: http://texasbeyondhistory.net/
The Virtual Museum of Texas Cultural Heritage: https://tbh.laits.utexas.edu/
Texas State Historical Association: www.Tshaonline.org
The Portal to Texas History: https://texashistory.unt.edu/
Texas State Library and Archives Commission: https://www.tsl.texas.gov/
Lesson plans, resources, and games: www.teachingtexas.org
Texas General Land Office: http://www.glo.texas.gov/
Large collection of Texas maps: http://www.lib.utexas.edu/maps/historical/history_texas.html
Daily "this day in Texas history" emails: https://texasdaybyday.com/
Primary sources: https://tshaonline.org/lone-star-history-links/1054
Texas Heritage Trail Regions: http://texastimetravel.com/
Texas Highways free quarterly *Texas Events Calendar/Wildflower Brochure*: www.texashighways.com/freepubs

General Texas History Museums
Institute of Texan Cultures – San Antonio
The Bryan Museum - Galveston
Old Red Museum – Dallas
Bullock Texas State History Museum – Austin
Panhandle-Plains Historical Museum - Canyon
Museum of North Texas History - Wichita Falls

Texas Artists and Art Museums
Elisabet Ney Museum in Hyde Park - Austin (sculptor)
Sid Richardson Museum - Fort Worth (Western Art)
Amon Carter Museum - Fort Worth
Frank Reaugh: http://www.hrc.utexas.edu/collections/art/holdings/texas/reaugh/
Briscoe Western Art Museum – San Antonio
O'Henry House and Museum – San Antonio and Austin

SUPPLIES YOU'LL NEED FOR THIS CURRICULUM:

- Globe (inflatable works well)
- Texas road map
- 3-ring binder for each student
- Loose-leaf notebook paper
- Dividing tabs with pockets (label and divide sections according to units and/or activities)
- Colored pencils
- Scissors
- Ruler
- Computer with internet access
- U.S. and world atlas
- Access to copy machine

Please see a complete list of specific resources and supplies following each unit's list of suggested activities.

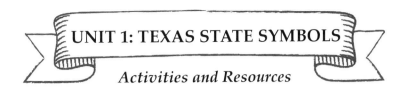

UNIT 1: TEXAS STATE SYMBOLS

Activities and Resources

⊹ INTRODUCTION ⊹

p. 7

VOCABULARY:

aspect, symbol, designate, native, emblem, valued, diverse, resolutions

VOCABULARY WINDOWPANE:

Complete the *Vocabulary Windowpane* using the vocabulary words listed above, and continue to add vocabulary words to your windowpanes throughout the unit. Write a vocabulary word in each "pane," define the word, and illustrate. (RB p. 33)

KWL:

Begin the *KWL Chart* on Texas State Symbols. Fill the "K" section with information you already know about the unit topic and then write down your thoughts about what you want to learn about the topic in the center "W" section. When you have finished the unit, complete the final "L" section with notes about what you learned. (RB p. 35)

COMPILING DATA:

Fill in the *A to Z Chart* about Texas State Symbols as you proceed through this unit. Come up with as many words beginning with each letter of the alphabet as you can which relate to the unit theme. It's o.k. to get creative, especially with letters such as x and z! (RB p. 21)

MATH:

Develop three possibilities for a new state symbol. Share those options with 20 other people. Based on their preferences, create a bar or pie graph to convey your results. You may create these graphs either by hand or with a computer chart software.

TEXAS FLAG & SIX FLAGS FLOWN OVER TEXAS

pp. 7-8

VOCABULARY:

perpendicular, horizontal, loyalty, purity (continue adding to your vocabulary windowpanes)

VENN DIAGRAM:

Select two of the six flags that have flown over Texas. Make a copy of the *Double Venn Diagram* template, and above each circle draw a picture of each of the flags. Compare the common characteristics (in overlapping areas) and differences between the two flags (make sure to include the dates that each served as the official flag). (RB p. 23)

ART:

Create a Texas flag mosaic using cut up pieces of magazine pictures (the pictures you select should match the correct color scheme). Sketch the Lone Star flag, then glue the torn or cut magazine picture pieces in the appropriate color area.

LOOK IT UP:

Name the Republic of Texas senator who introduced the Lone Star Flag to Congress on December 28th, 1838. (*Answer:* AG p. 103)

TEXAS PLEDGE AND STATE SEAL

p. 9

VOCABULARY:

pledge, allegiance, indivisible, instituted, affixed, adopted, reverse

MEMORY:

Memorize the *Texas Pledge*.

WRITING:

After reading the description of the reverse side of the seal, explain in your own words the design and its meaning.

COPY WORK:

Copy the *Texas Pledge* in a black marker, using your best writing. Then use colored pencils to lightly color the Lone Star flag over the writing, leaving a transparent effect.

THE STATE SONG

p. 9

VOCABULARY:

empire, radiance, tyrant, splendor, destiny

COPY WORK:

Copy the lyrics to all verses of the Texas State Song: "Texas, Our Texas." Decorate your copy work with pictures illustrating the meanings of the pledge and lyrics. Here is one source:

http://www.lsjunction.com/song.htm

LOOK IT UP:

In 1959, the lyrics "largest and grandest" were changed to "boldest and grandest." Why was this change in the lyrics necessary? (*Answer*: AG p. 103)

TEXAS STATE SYMBOLS

p. 10

VOCABULARY:

gem, reptile, mammal

COMPILING DATA:

How well do you know Texans and Texas? Complete the *Other Texas Symbols* activity. First, lightly pencil in your guess for these official state symbols. Check your answers, then note and illustrate the correct answer in each box. (RB p. 43; *Answers*: AG p. 105)

WRITING:

After you complete the *Introduction Math Activity* (p. 11) and determine your results, propose the adoption of a new state symbol and explain why and how it represents Texas. Research to whom and where to send your proposal and draft in a letter format. If it's a great idea, mail and submit it!

SCIENCE/COOKING:

Try your hand at making the state dish: chili. We've included a delicious recipe! (AG p. 91)

ART:

Select one (or more) of the suggested *Texas Symbol Art Projects* which depict official state symbols and create a masterpiece. (RB p. 44)

LOOK IT UP:

What is the Texas state bread? Find a recipe and try it for supper tonight with your chili! (AG p. 103)

UNIT TEST:

Complete the *Symbol Unit Test*. (RB pp. 116-17; *Answers*: AG p. 101)

SUGGESTED READING:
Miss Lady Bird's Wildflowers by Kathi Appelt
Legend of the Bluebonnet by Tomie dePaola
L is for Lonestar: A Texas Alphabet by Carol Crane
Armadillo Rodeo by Jan Brett
The Adventures of Arnie Armadillo (Texas State Symbols)
by Kathy Gause

ART TO EXPLORE:
Bluebonnet Paintings by Julian Onderdonk
Mockingbird Art by John James Audubon
The Bronco Buster bronze sculpture by Frederic Remington
The Bolter by Charles M. Russell

WEBSITES:
Texas State Symbols: https://www.tsl.texas.gov/ref/abouttx/symbols.html
More Texas State Symbols: www.statesymbolsusa.org/states/united-states/texas
State Seal of Texas:
www.sos.state.tx.us/statdoc/seal.shtml *and* www.lsjunction.com/seal.htm
Texas Flags and Symbols: texasalmanac.com/topics/flags-symbols
Texas Recipes: http://www.texascooking.com/

MUSIC AND SONGS TO LEARN
"Texas, Our Texas" by W. Marsh and G. Wright
"Deep in the Heart of Texas" by J. Hershey and D. Swander
"The Eyes of Texas Are Upon You" by J. Sinclair

Twenty Questions and Memory Game Suggestions:

mockingbird, 9-banded armadillo, chili, pecan tree, bluebonnet, pan de campo (cowboy bread), Guadalupe bass, Mexican free-tailed bat, longhorn, horned lizard, Lightning whelk shell, prickly pear cactus, cowboy boots, Lone Star flag, American flag, state seal

PLACES TO VISIT:

Lady Bird Johnson Wildflower Center - Austin
Congress Avenue Bridge - Austin, to see the Mexican Free-Tailed Bats
Daily Longhorn Cattle Drive - Historic Fort Worth Stockyards
Lone Star Monument and Historical Flag Park - Conroe
Bluebonnet Trails - Ennis and the Texas Hill Country (usually in April)
The Texas State Capitol - Austin
River Bend Nature Center - Wichita Falls
Bluebonnet Festival - Chappell Hill, Burnet, Kemp, & Natalia (April)
And of course, your children will suggest an (ahem) historic trip to **Six Flags Over Texas**!

SUPPLY LIST:
- old magazines, scissors, glue
- recipe ingredients for *Chili*
- various materials for *Other State Symbols Art Activities*
- ingredients for *State Bread*
- black marker

WRITING
PROMPT
PAGE 113

Texans love to take annual family pictures in the bluebonnet fields!

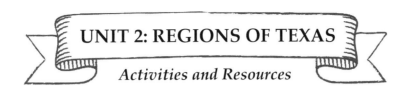

UNIT 2: REGIONS OF TEXAS

Activities and Resources

OUR PLACE IN THE WORLD

pp. 11-13

VOCABULARY:

region, climate, landform, latitude, longitude, fertile, equator, hemisphere, eroding, atmosphere, intersect, parallel, crust

VOCABULARY WINDOWPANE:

Complete the *Vocabulary Windowpane* using the vocabulary words above, and continue to add vocabulary words throughout the unit. (RB p. 33)

KWL:

Begin the *KWL Chart* on the Regions of Texas. Once you have completed the unit, don't forget to add notes about what you learned in the final "L" column. (RB p. 35)

COMPILING DATA:

Fill in the *A to Z Chart* about Texas Regions as you proceed through this unit. (RB p. 21)

MATH:

Complete the **On the Road Again** Distance and Measurement Activity.
(RB p. 45-46; *Answers*: AG p. 105)

GEOGRAPHY:

• *What's My Name?* Riddles (RB p. 47-48; *Answers*: AG p. 105)
• *Bingo Latitude and Longitude* Activity (RB p. 51-52; *Answers*: AG p. 105)
• *Ordering Home by Size* Activity (RB p. 53-54) Cut out each rectangle, adding your personal geographic information in the blanks. Mix them up, then put in order by size. For fun, affix magnets to the back of each label and arrange on your refrigerator or metal cookie sheet.

CRAFT:

Where Do I Live? Geography Activity. Cut incrementally larger sizes of construction paper into rectangles. Fold the two edges of each rectangle in towards the middle, so that they meet like double doors. With a dot of glue, attach the construction paper rectangles, one inside the other, so that when they are closed, only the largest one is seen and can be opened. On the outside of the biggest set of "double doors," label the main cover *Universe* and draw stars, moon, planets, etc. (For a nice effect, use a white crayon on black or dark blue paper.) Label the next set of double doors *Earth*, tracing around a small dish for a circle. Continue using the shape tracers (RB p. 49) to create pages for *North America*, *United States*, and *Texas*. The last rectangles should be the *residential city* and *home* or *bedroom*, although *county* and *neighborhood* may be added if desired. Note: there will be a slit down the middle of each picture (other than the final rectangle), where the "doors" meet. (Example: AG p. 22)

MAP SKILLS:

First, label the rivers on the Texas River map (RB p. 15). Then, on the Texas map outline, add these rivers to the map yourself; label the Gulf of Mexico and the border states. (RB p. 9)

COPY WORK:

Copy the Sam Houston quote and illustrate with a beautiful Texas landscape. (AG p. 97)

LOOK IT UP:

Find the origins of the names of three major Texas rivers.

REGIONS OF TEXAS

South Texas Plains

pp. 14-15

VOCABULARY:

subtropical, mild, citrus, annual, resacas, ox-bow lake, channel, silt, marsh, delta, tropical, habitat, conservation, industry, caracara

GEOGRAPHY:

A. On the *Texas Regions Map*, color the South Texas Plains region yellow and label five cities. (RB p. 13)

B. Fill in the *Quadrant Chart* and draw pictures of regional native plants and animals. (RB p. 55)

WRITING:

Having read *On the Road Again* in the previous section, write your own *On the Road Again* story and develop a similar quiz for another student (or parent) to complete.

COPY WORK:

Research names of famous people from the South Texas Plains Region. Copy a quote about or by one of these well-known Texans. Add an illustration of that famous individual.

COOKING:

Try the *King Ranch Chicken* recipe for your family dinner tonight. (AG p. 92)

LOOK IT UP:

The King Ranch cattle brand was first registered in 1869. Find what the brand looks like, copy it, and see if you can find out what the image symbolizes. There are several theories—add yours to the mix! (*Answer*: AG p. 103)

Prairies and Lakes

p. 16

VOCABULARY:

reservoir, prairie, fossilized, ecoregions

GEOGRAPHY:

A. On the *Texas Regions Map*, color the Prairies and Lakes region green and label five cities. (RB p. 13)

B. Fill in the *Quadrant Chart* and draw pictures of regional native plants and animals. (RB p. 55)

COPY WORK:

Research names of famous people from the Prairies and Lakes Region. Copy a quote about or by one of these well-known Texans. Add an illustration of that famous individual.

WRITING:

Write a *haiku* poem about this region. (Easy directions for writing haiku can be found online.)

SCIENCE:

Begin a collection of soil samples using labeled plastic baggies. Start with samples from your area, and continue your collection as you travel to different parts of Texas, or even the U.S. or world. Compare color, texture, and how the soil reacts to moisture. If you have access to a microscope, investigate further and draw what you see.

LOOK IT UP:

The Brazos River runs through this region and was originally called *Rio de los Brazos de Dios*. Translate this Spanish phrase to English. Why do you think the river was given that name? (*Answer*: AG p. 103)

pp. 17-18

VOCABULARY:

abundant, basin, canyons, plateau, wetland, artifacts, culture, inhabitants, remote, arroyo, tinaja, grazing

GEOGRAPHY:

A. On the *Texas Regions Map*, color the Big Bend region red and label five cities. (RB p. 13)

B. Fill in the *Quadrant Chart* and draw pictures of regional native plants and animals. (RB p. 55)

COPY WORK:

Research names of famous people from the Big Bend Region. Copy a quote about or by one of these well-known Texans. Add an illustration of that famous individual.

COOKING:

This region is well-known for area chili cook-offs. Purchase 6-8 different types of hot peppers. Compare by color, size, shape, weight, smell, and if you are really brave . . . taste and rank by heat!

SCIENCE:

Put one-half cup of water in four identical containers. Place one outside in the sun, one in the shade, one on the kitchen counter, and one in the refrigerator. Measure evaporation rates daily and chart results. How do you think the arid climate in the Big Bend region affects the evaporation rate and available water sources?

WRITING:

Have you ever heard of the Marfa Lights? People have been seeing mysterious lights in the sky just east of Marfa, Texas, for over 100 years. Do a little research on this phenomenon, then write a first-person story about seeing these eerie lights. Illustrate, of course!

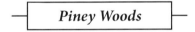

p. 19

VOCABULARY:

swamps, ecological, timber, lumber, humid

GEOGRAPHY:

A. On the *Texas Regions Map*, color the Piney Woods region brown and label five cities. (RB p. 13)

B. Fill in the *Quadrant Chart* and draw pictures of native plants and animals. (RB p. 55)

COPY WORK:

Research names of famous people from the Piney Woods Region. Copy a quote about or by one of these well-known Texans. Add an illustration of that famous individual.

CRAFT:

Find trees native to *your* region and use a crayon to make rubbings. Label each tree rubbing. Are any trees in your area also native to the Piney Woods?

MATH:

Predict which room in your home has the most materials made from wood and estimate how many total interior items in your home are products from the lumber industry. Check your prediction and estimate. How close were your guesses to the actual results?

LOOK IT UP:

The city of Huntsville is found in the Piney Woods region. What university is located there? (*Answer*: AG p. 103)

Hill Country

p. 20

VOCABULARY:

granite, limestone, bedrock, aquifer, springs, irrigation, caverns, spelunker, domes, uplifts, grasslands, woodlands, urban, quarry, emerge

GEOGRAPHY:

A. On the *Texas Regions Map*, color the Hill Country region pink and label five cities. (RB p. 13)

B. Fill in the *Quadrant Chart* and draw pictures of regional native plants and animals. (RB p. 55)

COPY WORK:

Research names of famous people from the Hill Country Region. Copy a quote about or by one of these well-known Texans. Add an illustration of that famous individual.

COOKING:

Make *Spaetzle*, a traditional dish made by many Germans who settled in the area. (AG p. 92)

LOOK IT UP:

Bedrock mortars can be found at Enchanted Rock. What are/were these windows to the past? Who made them, and when? (*Answer*: AG p. 103)

Gulf Coast

pp. 21-22

VOCABULARY:

sediment, barrier islands, bays, estuaries, encompasses, seaports, petrochemicals, aerospace, copious, migrating, elevation, inland, seawall

GEOGRAPHY:

A. On the *Texas Regions Map*, color the Gulf Coast region blue and label five cities. (RB p. 13)

B. Fill in the *Quadrant Chart* and draw pictures of regional native plants and animals. (RB p. 55)

COPY WORK:

Research names of famous people from the Gulf Coast Region. Copy a quote about or by one of these well-known Texans. Add an illustration of that famous individual.

COOKING:

Try the *Shrimp Gumbo* recipe, a Gulf Coast favorite. (AG p. 93)

LOOK IT UP:

What is the *Gulf Intracoastal Waterway*? How far does it extend? (*Answer*: AG p. 103)

Panhandle Plains

p. 23

VOCABULARY:

plain, escarpment, playa lake, evaporate, wind power

GEOGRAPHY:

A. On the *Texas Regions Map*, color the Panhandle Plains region orange and label five cities. (RB p. 13)

B. Fill in the *Quadrant Chart* and draw pictures of regional native plants and animals. (RB p. 55)

COPY WORK:

Find five interesting and unique names of cities in each region and copy in your best handwriting. Illustrate with a picture of a landmark that can be found in one of those cities.

WRITING:

Write a persuasive letter home, convincing a family member to visit the Panhandle Plains.

MATH:

Measure the approximate longest and shortest distances across each Texas region on your region map with your ruler. Then, for fun, see if you can calculate approximate mileage using an official Texas map with a mileage scale.

NUTRITION:

Investigate the different cuts of beef and where on the cow they are located.

NATIVE PLANTS AND ANIMALS

pp. 24-26

VOCABULARY:

invertebrates, intentionally, docile, dwindling, endangered species, extinct, threatened species, invasive, ancestors, forbs, kudzu

SCIENCE:

A: Buy crunchy chocolate chip cookies. Become a paleontologist and use a toothbrush, a small paintbrush, and a toothpick as your tools. Try to "retrieve" the chocolate chips without damaging them.

B: Make your own Plaster of Paris fossils. Follow directions to mix plaster. Search for animal tracks or use different types of leaves to press your own imprints.

WRITING:

A. Choose an endangered Texas plant or animal. Research and write a report including its natural habitat, how many of the species still survive, what caused the numbers to decrease, and what is currently being done to protect it.

B. Texas is home to over 5,000 varieties of native flowering plants and many have interesting and descriptive names. *Bluebonnet, Mexican Hat, Indian Paintbrush* ... Research and make a list of ten other unique Texas wildflower names. Draw a "literal" picture of the flower name (for example: a bonnet [hat] that is blue, and next to that, illustrate an actual bluebonnet flower).

LOOK IT UP:

What is the Latin word for the nine-banded armadillo? What is the Latin name's literal translation? (*Answer*: AG p. 103)

UNIT TEST:

Complete the *Texas Regions Unit Test*. (RB pp. 118-19; *Answers*: AG p. 101)

EXTRA OPTIONAL ACTIVITIES:

- *Sorting Texas Regions* Activity (RB p. 57; Answers: AG p. 105)
- *Look It Up:* Make a chart with information on average household income, rainfall, temperature, and/or population within each region.
- *Art*: Create a three-dimensional sculpture of your favorite region depicting terrain and native flora and fauna. Using foamboard as the base, cut in the shape of the region. Use modeling dough or sculpting clay to form the landscape.
- *Map Vocabulary Quiz* (RB p. 58; *Answers*: AG p. 105)
- *Mapping Practice* (RB p. 56)

```
┌─────────────────────────────────────────────┐
│                ART TO EXPLORE:               │
│   Big Bend (series of paintings) by Alexandre Hogue   │
│        Big Bend Landscapes by Dennis Blagg           │
│        Hilltop Gardens by Dalhart Windberg           │
│   Hill Country Texas Landscape by Porfirio Salinas    │
│  Galveston Wharf with Cotton Bales by Julius Stockfleth │
│        Caprock Canyons #2 by Randy Bacon             │
│    West Texas Landscape by Harry Peyton Carnohan      │
│      West Texas Photographs by Wyman Meinzer          │
└─────────────────────────────────────────────┘
```

SUGGESTED READING:

The Adventures of Arnie Armadillo (Region Series) by Kathy Gause

Focus on Texas: History and Geography by Richard Sorenson

Roadside Geology of Texas by Darwin Spearing (teens/adults)

Texas: A Historical Atlas by Ray A. Stephens

Historic Houston and How to See It: 100 Years and 100 Miles of Day Trips by Lucinda Freeman (teens/adults)

Texas Almanac: Annual publication of Texas State Historical Association. Up-to-date information about Texas' regions, features, economy, and much more!

Official Guide to Texas State Parks and Historic Sites edited by Laurence Parent

WEBSITES:

Texas Almanac: www.texasalmanac.com - learn all about Texas's geographic and land regions, weather, record-setting features, and events.

Texas Parks and Wildlife Department: https://tpwd.texas.gov/kids/about_texas/regions/ - teaches about the vegetation, wildlife, rainfall, and other characteristics of each region.

Historical Commission: www.thc.state.tx.us/explore-texas - learn about the natural, cultural, and historic resources found within each Texas region.

Tour Texas: www.tourtexas.com - browse the cities and attractions located within each Texas region; order free travel brochures.

Native Plant Society of Texas: www.npsot.org/wp/

Texas Heritage Trail Regions: texastimetravel.com

Texas Forestry Museum: www.texasforestrymuseum.com/kids/activities

Twenty Questions and Memory Game Suggestions:

Panhandle Plains, Gulf Coast, Hill Country, South Texas Plains, Piney Woods, Big Bend Country, Prairies and Lakes, aquifer, playa lake, canyon, tinaja, marsh, caracara, granite, barrier island

WRITING
PROMPT
PAGE 115

PLACES TO VISIT

South Texas Plains:
1. *World Birding Center* - Mission
2. *Choke Canyon State Park* - Calliham
3. *Goliad State Park (Mission), Presidio La Bahía, and Fannin Memorial* - Goliad
4. *Fannin Battleground State Historic Site* - Fannin

Prairies and Lakes:
1. *Dinosaur Valley State Park* - Glen Rose
2. *Fossil Rim Wildlife Center* - Glen Rose
3. *Mineral Wells Fossil Park* - Mineral Wells
4. *Lake Mineral Wells State Park and Trailway*
5. *Washington-on-the-Brazos State Historic Site* - Washington, Tx.

Big Bend Country:
1. *Big Bend National Park*
2. *Monahans Sandhills State Park* - Monahans
3. *Guadalupe Mountains National Park* - Salt Flat
4. *Balmorhea State Park* - Toyahvale
5. *Davis Mountains State Park* - Fort Davis
6. *McDonald Observatory* - Fort Davis
7. *Marfa (try to see the Marfa Lights!)*
8. *Chihuahuan Desert Research Institute* - Fort Davis

Piney Woods:
1. *Caddo Lake State Park* - Karnack
2. *Big Thicket National Preserve* - Kountz
3. *Davy Crockett National Forest's Big Slough Wilderness Area*
4. *Sam Houston National Forest* - New Waverly
5. *Caddo Mounds State Historic Site* - Alto
6. *Mission Tejas State Park* - Grapeland
7. *Texas Railroad State Park* - Rusk and Palestine State Parks
8. *Pineywoods Native Plant Center* - Nacogdoches

Hill Country:
1. *Cascade Caverns* - Boerne
2. *Nature cruises on Lake Buchanan*
3. *Enchanted Rock State Natural Area* - Fredericksburg
4. *Lost Maples State Park* - Vanderpool
5. *Garner State Park* - Concan
6. *Longhorn and Kickapoo Caverns State Parks* - Burnet *and* Brackettville
7. *Lyndon B. Johnson State Park and Historic Site* - Stonewall
8. *Natural Bridge Caverns* - San Antonio
9. *Caverns of Sonora* - Sonora
10. *Innerspace Caverns* - Georgetown

Gulf Coast:
1. *Padre Island National Seashore* - Corpus Christi
2. *Armand Bayou Nature Center* - Pasadena
3. *Brazos Bend State Park* - Needville
4. *Sea Center Texas* - Lake Jackson
5. *Texas State Aquarium* - Corpus Christi
6. *Aransas National Wildlife Refuge* - Austwell
7. *Matagorda County Birding Nature Center* - Bay City
8. *Stephen F. Austin State Park and San Felipe State Historic Site* - San Felipe

Panhandle Plains:
1 *Palo Duro Canyon State Park* - Canyon
2 *Caprock Canyons State Park* – Quitaque
3. *Sibley Nature Center* - Midland

Where Do I Live? Activity

SUPPLY LIST:
- plastic baggies
- 6-8 types of peppers
- 4 identical clear containers
- crunchy chocolate chip cookies
- toothbrush, paintbrush, toothpick
- plaster of paris
- foam board
- modeling dough or sculpting clay
- recipe ingredients for *King Ranch Chicken*
- recipe ingredients for *Spaetzle*
- recipe ingredients for *Shrimp Gumbo*
- construction paper and glue

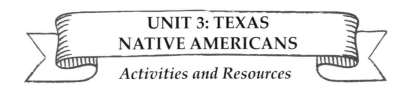

ORIGINS

p. 27

VOCABULARY:

archeologists, corridor

VOCABULARY WINDOWPANE:

Complete the *Vocabulary Windowpane* using the vocabulary words above, and continue to add vocabulary words throughout the unit. (RB p. 33)

KWL:

Begin the *KWL Chart* regarding Texas Native Americans. Once you have completed the unit, don't forget to add notes about what you learned in the final "L" column. (RB p. 35)

MATH:

Timeline: this can serve as a year-long continuous activity. Make as many copies as needed and cut the paper along the dotted lines. Tape together to make one long strip. Write the year(s) in the oval in the first arrow and add known information about events occurring in the world, U.S., and Texas. Begin with the year 1 A.D. What was happening in the rest of the world? In the U.S.? In Texas? Continue by adding important dates from each unit. (RB p. 41)

COMPILING DATA:

Fill in the *A to Z Chart* about Texas Native Americans as you proceed through this unit. (RB p. 21)

GEOGRAPHY:

Interview older family members and find out what you can about where your ancestors came from and when they arrived in the U.S. and Texas. Look up the meaning of your surname (last name) and create a simple family tree going back at least three generations or more, if you can.

LOOK IT UP:

Look at a map and notice how close Alaska and Siberia are at their nearest point. Assuming the theory that the first Americans found their way to this continent by crossing the Bering Strait is correct, how many miles were eventually crossed by these families and their descendants from where they arrived in Alaska all the way until they reached Texas? (*Answer*: AG p. 103)

EARLY PREHISTORIC INDIANS

p. 28

VOCABULARY:

decodable, relics, atlatl, supplement, metates, manos, chert, hunter-gatherers, domesticated, maize, temples, edible, flint

PHYSICAL SCIENCE:

How fast does your "Ice Age" progress? Try this experiment: using four clear plastic cups, fill each with the same amount of water. Label the first cup *Pure H_2O*. Add 1 tsp. of table salt to the second cup, 2 tsp. salt to the third, and 3 tsp. salt to the fourth. Label the other cups accordingly, using the formula *H_2O + 1 tsp. NaCl*, etc. Place the cups in your freezer in a stable location. Check hourly and note the state of the water. How long did it take the first cup to get icy? To get slushy? To freeze solid? How about the salty water? Does salt, and the amount of salt, change the freezing point of the water? Does the salty water ever freeze solid? Do the four cups melt at the same rate?

WRITING:

Complete the *Artifact Acrostic* (RB p. 60) For each letter in the word "Artifacts," write a word or words that have some connection to the word itself. (i.e. A=archeologist, R=remains) OR write an eight line poem about artifacts, with each line starting with the corresponding letter.

ANIMAL SCIENCE:

Using the *Triple Venn Diagram*, compare the mammoth, mastodon, and elephant. (RB p. 25)

CRAFTS:

Research Native American painted symbols found in Texas caves and rock overhangs. Re-create some of these pictographs (and maybe some of your own) by painting with earthy colors on a paper sack.

LOOK IT UP:

The Alibates Quarry in the Texas Panhandle was a popular place to find what resource, often used by Native Americans to make tools and weapons? (*Answer*: AG p. 103)

THE BUFFALO

pp. 29-31

VOCABULARY:

herbivore, pelt, pishkun, phosphorous, protein, sustenance, pemmican, rawhide, sweat lodge, ladle, tendons, dung, gored, imposter, bridle

COMPILING DATA:

Complete the *Buffalo Part Chart*. (RB p. 59) In the first column, draw a picture of one body part of the buffalo. In the second column, label the body part and in the third column, list the ways the Native Americans utilized that part of the buffalo to assist with their daily chores, weapons, ornamentation, etc. Body parts might include, but are not limited to: horns, bladder, stomach, brains, skull, hooves, dung, tongue, hair, sinew, and meat. You'll enjoy this interesting site dedicated to the topic: **http://americanbison.si.edu/american-bison-and-american-indian-nations/**

COPY WORK:

Copy this entry about buffalo usage written by a chronicler of the Coronado expedition. (AG p. 97)

ECONOMICS:

Research the buffalo nickel. When was it changed and why? What is the value of a buffalo nickel today? What other coins have changed over time? What could you buy with a buffalo nickel in 1920? What can you buy with a nickel today? Here is one site to calculate inflation: (*Answer*: AG p. 106)

http://www.dollartimes.com/calculators/inflation.htm

WRITING:

Write a story about a buffalo hunt, BUT from the point of view of the buffalo.

COOKING:

You'll have to do some research, but find a local store that carries ground bison. Try making your own buffalo burgers. How do the taste and texture compare to regular hamburger meat?

ART:

Look up Remington and Russell paintings depicting buffalo. How would you describe the style differences of each artist? Which do you prefer?

LOOK IT UP:

How fast can a buffalo run? You'll be surprised! (*Answer*: AG p. 103)

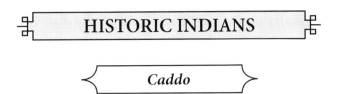

Caddo

pp. 32-34

VOCABULARY:

descendants, ample, unhusked, breechcloth, sophisticated, gourds, turquoise, trotlines, hamlets, succotash, bois d'arc, moccasins

ECONOMICS:

The Caddo often traded goods with the Spanish. An old document from the 1780s gave examples of goods the Spanish traded for deerskins. Here are some samples of the rate of exchange:

1 hatchet = 5 deerskins   1 folding knife = 1 deerskin

1 musket = 30 deerskins   1 1/3 yards of cloth = 20 deerskins

1 lance = 10 deerskins   1 metal bracelet = 1 deerskin

Rate of exchange is usually based on the perceived value of items. Looking at these examples, what types of goods were most valuable to this particular group of Indians, and why?

Compare the value to today's rate of exchange for these goods in terms of U.S. dollars. Are these objects more or less valuable to most Americans today? Why?

COMPILING DATA:

Begin the *Chart of Texas Tribes* and continue throughout this unit for each tribe. (RB pp. 61-62)

LEGENDS:

There are many stories and legends about the coyote in Caddo folklore. Find a few to read, then write your own tale about that silly coyote.

WRITING:

Similar to the Egyptians, the Caddo were buried with objects used in daily life. If you were to plan your own burial (when you are very, very old, of course!), what items would be included in your final resting place and why? How might those objects differ from those of the Caddo, and why?

CRAFTS:

The Caddo were famous for their beautiful pottery. Find some examples of Caddo pottery online and try your hand at creating a similar object with air-dry or self-hardening clay.

Karankawa

pp. 35-36

VOCABULARY:

cannibalism, nomads, dugout, invaluable, wigwams, middens, lances, tomahawks, shaman, fearsome, cradleboards, transition, mitotes, tambourine, javelina, tar, cedar, refuse (noun), Spanish moss

COPY WORK:

Try to find online a firsthand description of the Karankawa. Copy and illustrate.

MATH:

The Karankawa enjoyed wrestling matches. Set up an arm wrestling tournament. Time the number of minutes or seconds for each bout from beginning to end. How many minutes/seconds were the longest and shortest bouts? What is the difference between the two? What is the average duration of all of the bouts? What is the median time of all the bouts?

WRITING:

Many settlers along the Texas coastline learned to keep nightgowns or sheets on their clotheslines to scare away the superstitious Karankawa, who believed the flapping fabric to be ghosts. Write a spooky story set in that time period.

SCIENCE:

Research, sketch, and describe five types of shells found on Texas beaches. Come up with various ways the Karankawa might have made use of each shell as some kind of tool.

LOOK IT UP:

The word cactus comes from the Greek word *kaktos*. What does *kaktos* literally mean in English? (*Answer:* AG p. 103)

Coahuiltecan

pp. 37-38

VOCABULARY:

foraging, thicket, seines, tumpline, consume, autonomous, willow, sotol, lechuguilla, maguey, symmetry, stamina, geographical

WRITING:

Write an obituary for the now-extinct Coahuiltecan Indians. Be sure to include what they did, the years they lived, and how they died.

COOKING:

See if you can find fresh tunas (the seasonal fruit of the prickly pear cactus) in the produce section of your grocery store. Be sure to carefully remove the outer rind before you eat it. If they are out of season, then look for a jar of napolitos (made from the pads of the prickly pear cactus).

CRAFTS:

Create a cactus garden! Find a variety of flat and fairly thin oval rocks. Paint each rock to look like cactus (don't forget the spines!). "Plant" your cactus rocks in soil, sticking straight up, in a small clay flower pot (you can paint and decorate the flower pot, too).

LOOK IT UP:

How did the Native Americans pick and prepare the prickly pear without getting their fingers full of thorns? Some animals eat the fruit of the prickly pear. How do they do that without getting a mouth full of thorns? (*Answer:* AG p. 103)

Comanche

pp. 39-40

VOCABULARY:

displaced, comancheria, fire pit, travois, leggings, buckskin, tinklers, parfleche, quiver, battle axe, pictograph, mode, breeding, supernatural, councils, alliances, ambush, scalps

MATH:

With the arrival of the horse, the ability to chase buffalo improved. What is the time difference between walking a mile versus riding a horse? How long would it take to walk across Texas? How long would it take to ride a horse across Texas? How long would it take to drive across Texas in a car today? Measure a line east-west across the widest part of Texas to estimate the distance. (*Answer:* AG p. 106)

WRITING:

Read *The Legend of the Bluebonnet*. Write a paragraph about your most prized possession.

COOKING:

Taste-test beef jerky. List twenty adjectives to describe the taste, texture, appearance, smell, size, and quality.

CRAFTS:

Look at pictures online of Comanche war paint. Decorate your face accordingly!

LOOK IT UP:

In 2010, a man walked the perimeter of Texas. How many miles might that be? How fast do you think he walked? How long would it take to walk the perimeter of Texas at that speed? (*Answer*: AG p. 103)

P.E.:

Play the popular Comanche *Bone Game*. Two teams face each other. While one team sings or beats a drum, the other team passes a small bone (or button) from member to member as they try to distract the other team. When the music stops, the other team guesses who has the bone!

WHAT IF?:

What if the Comanche had never gained access to horses? How might their culture and lifestyle have been different?

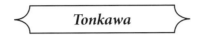

Tonkawa

pp. 41-42

VOCABULARY:

scarce, jerky, sinew, breastplate, choker, pendant, notable, firearms, tallow, manifestations, refuge, adornment

P.E.:

The Tonkawas, even the women and children, prided themselves on strength. Gather three or four friends and chart your physical abilities such as pushups, sit ups, pull ups, running, etc.

SCIENCE:

Wolves were sacred to the Tonkawa. Research the estimated numbers of wolves living in the United States today. Do they still exist in the wild in Texas? Are they endangered, and if so, what is being done to protect them? (*Answer*: AG p. 106)

COPY WORK:

Wolves were sacred to not only the Tonkawa, but to other American Indian tribes as well. The Cherokee have a beautiful, old legend about two wolves. Copy it in your best handwriting and illustrate. (AG p. 97)

LOOK IT UP:

The Tonkawa occasionally helped a Texas law enforcement organization, especially against their enemy, the Comanche. What group did they assist? (*Answer*: AG p. 103)

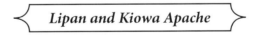

Lipan and Kiowa Apache

pp. 43-44

VOCABULARY:

dwelling, depicted, arbor, mulberry, rodents, agave, tunic, tanning, plume, arsenal, wickiup

WRITING:

Using only pictographs, write a story about a day in the life of a Lipan or Kiowa Apache.

COOKING:

The Apache ate many types of roots. What root vegetables are available in your grocery store? Choose one or two you have never tried, look up a fun recipe, and taste them.

CRAFTS:

Construct a small teepee using chopsticks and paper or a life-size teepee using bamboo or garden stakes and an old sheet. Be sure to decorate your teepee with traditional symbols. The Apache women could erect their teepees in three minutes. What is the fastest you can set up yours?

LOOK IT UP:

Apache women sometimes smoked bees from their hive to obtain that special treat: honey. Many people today enjoy beekeeping. How many pounds of honey are typically produced by a hive each year? (*Answer*: AG p. 103)

Jumano

pp. 45-46

VOCABULARY:

mesquite, pueblo, adobe, semi-permanent, pigment, middlemen, wampum, vague, rawhide, ponchos

MATH:

Estimate how many kernels are on one ear of corn. Then count them—how close was your estimate?

WRITING:

A very mysterious story exists about a nun, Sister María of Ágreda, also known as the "Lady in Blue." During the 1620s, Jumanos reported seeing a lady dressed in blue, later assumed to be Sister María, hundreds of times in Texas, New Mexico, and Arizona. She wore the traditional Franciscan robes, with a blue cloak and black veil, teaching the Indians about Christianity and encouraging them to be baptized. The mysterious part? Sister María never left Ágreda, which was in Spain! Even more interesting . . . Sister María reported being "transported" to speak to the Jumanos. Read more about this fascinating story (or myth!) and decide for yourself. Write a short story about the *Lady in Blue*, from the perspective of a Jumano Indian. Then, if you are skeptical, come up with an explanation of why and how these stories began.

GEOGRAPHY:

Find Ágreda, Spain, on a map. Measure the distance between Ágreda and West Texas. How many miles would Sister María have "traveled" if the *Lady in Blue* story was true? Estimate how long the journey would take if she were to walk, bicycle, or fly in an airplane today. (*Answer*: AG p. 106)

CRAFTS:

The Jumano created jewelry, making the tribe popular with traders. String your own beads to design a necklace, bracelet, or anklet.

LOOK IT UP:

One group of Jumano Indians lived along the Rio Grande River. Exactly how long is the Rio Grande River, from its source in Colorado to its mouth at the Gulf of Mexico? (*Answer*: AG p. 103)

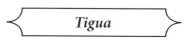

Tigua

pp. 47-48

VOCABULARY:

canal, hatchway, kiva, horno, revolt

CRAFT:

Construct a pueblo from an assortment of cereal, shoe, and other small boxes. Build ladders from balsa wood or popsicle sticks. Cut out doors and windows. Glue together and paint brown (textured spray paint adds a very realistic dimension to your pueblo).

WRITING:

A. Research and write about how cotton is used to make fabric. Include all steps from field to fabric.

B. Research the background for the legend of the "Three Sisters." Then write your own legend about how the trio of plants was given this unusual name.

SCIENCE:

Native Americans and others dyed their clothes for many years using natural colors found in plants. Buy a small portion of muslin. Cut in strips and soak fabric in plant dyes (you can find instructions for making natural dyes online). Try dyes made from beet juice, tea bags, frozen blueberries, onion peels, etc.

ART:

Use the *Comic Strip* template and illustrate how many Native Americans used the companion planting technique to grow the "Three Sisters" of corn, beans, and squash. (RB p. 37)

COOKING:

A. Cook the simple *Three Sisters Soup Recipe* for dinner tonight! (AG p. 94)

B. When the planting season is right for your area, try your hand at using companion planting to grow the "Three Sisters" of corn, beans, and squash.

LOOK IT UP:

The Tigua grew cotton and used it to make their clothes. The separation of the cotton fibers from the seeds could be very time consuming. Eventually, in 1793, a man invented a machine which could separate the fibers and seeds. What was the name of the machine and who was the inventor? (*Answer*: AG p. 103)

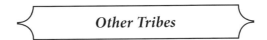

Other Tribes

p. 49

VOCABULARY:

census, migrant

WRITING:

Write a story about Texas Native Americans, interspersing ten words from the Cherokee language in your text. You might want to start with this website:

http://www.cherokee.org/AboutTheNation/Language/Dikaneisdi(WordList).aspx

MATH:

Do the math! Find the year of the following events and then calculate the number of years between the two events: (*Answers*: AG p. 106)

Columbus's First Voyage to the New World *and* **The Battle of the Alamo**

Coronado's Expedition Begins *and* **the First Spindletop Oil Gusher**

Pineda Maps the Gulf of Mexico *and* **Sam Houston is Elected Governor of Texas**

The Great Galveston Hurricane *and* **Man First Lands on the Moon**

WHAT IF?:

What if the Texas Native Americans had never been pushed out of Texas and into Indian Territory? How might our state look today? How might the presence of the tribes who once lived here affect our current culture and lifestyle?

LOOK IT UP:

Find ten cities, counties, or bodies of water in Texas named for Native American tribes or derived from Indian words.

ART:

A. Using the *Comic Strip* template, demonstrate a buffalo hunt from beginning to end. (RB p. 37)

B. Choose your favorite tribe and make a Native American Paper Doll (RB p. 63)

UNIT TEST:

Complete the *Native Americans of Texas Unit Test*. (RB p. 120-21; *Answers*: AG p. 101)

SUGGESTED READING:

Texas: Native Peoples by Mary Dodson Wade
The Sign of the Beaver by Elizabeth George Speare (historical fiction)
Joseph Bruchac has written many children's books and stories that tell traditional and non-fiction Native American stories. You'll find a list of his books here:
http://www.josephbruchac.com/published_books.html
The Indians of Texas by W. W. Newcomb, Jr. (teens/adults)
The Legend of the Bluebonnet by Tomie dePaola
The Legend of the Indian Paintbrush by Tomie dePaola
Learn About Texas Indians by Georg Zappler
Native American Tales and Activities by Mari Lu Robbins
Native American Legends and Activities by Mari Lu Robbins
Let's Remember Indians of Texas by Betsy Warren
The First Texans by Carolyn Mitchell Burnett
Cherokee A-B-C Coloring Book with Words in English and Cherokee by Daniel Pennington
The Buffalo and the Indians by Dorothy Hinshaw Patent

ur

WEBSITES:

Texas Native Americans: http://www.native-languages.org/texas.htm
Texas Native American history:
http://texasalmanac.com/topics/culture/american-indian/american-indian
Texas Indian Archaeology: http://www.texasbeyondhistory.net/
Cherokee Language:
http://www.cherokee.org/AboutTheNation/Language/Dikaneisdi(WordList).aspx
Rate of goods' exchange between Caddo and Spanish:
http://www.crt.state.la.us/dataprojects/archaeology/LosAdaes/_html/2_10_00.htm

Twenty Questions and Memory Game Suggestions:

Karankawa, Caddo, Comanche, Coahuiltecan, Tonkawa, Jumano, Tigua, Apache, Cherokee, Alabama-Coushatta, Kickapoo, Wichita, travois, prickly pear cactus, the "Three Sisters," javelina, buffalo, quiver, atlatl, shaman, adobe, mesquite

IT'S ABOUT TIME! Game Suggestions:

Prehistoric Texas Indians (before 1500), Caddo make contact with early explorers (1541), Comanche documented in Texas (1743), Tigua arrive in Texas (1682), Karankawa meet Cabeza de Vaca (1529), Coahuiltecans meet Cabeza de Vaca (1533-34), Cherokee and other Texas tribes removed from Texas (1839)

WRITING
PROMPT
PAGE 117

MUSIC AND SONGS:

Native American Instruments
www.teachervision.com/
native-americans/
native-american-instruments

Make your own instruments, find music online, and play along!

Make your own teepee!

PLACES TO VISIT:

Caddo Mounds State Historic Site - Alto
The Museum of Big Bend Country - Alpine
Seminole Canyon State Park and Historic Site - Comstock
Kwahadi Museum of the American Indian - Amarillo
Alabama-Coushatta Tribe of Texas - Livingston
Ysleta del Sur Pueblo Tigua Indian Cultural Center - El Paso
White Shaman Preserve – Comstock
Paint Rock Site – Paint Rock
Waco Mammoth National Monument – Waco

SUPPLY LIST:

- thermometer
- clear cups
- ice
- brown paper sack
- ground bison
- ingredients for *Three Sisters Soup* recipe
- air-dry or self-hardening clay
- stop watch
- prickly pear tunas
- beef jerky assortment
- face paint
- root vegetables
- chopsticks or large bamboo sticks; paper or an old sheet
- ears of corn
- beads and material to string them
- assortment of boxes
- paint (textured, if possible)
- 1/2 yard of muslin cut into strips
- plants to use for dye

Using the comic strip to review his knowledge of the Karankawas.

TIMELINE OF WORLD EXPLORATION

pp. 51-53

VOCABULARY:

Renaissance, fund, circumnavigate, inhabitants, colonization, rebelled, conquistador, empire

VOCABULARY WINDOWPANE:

Complete the *Vocabulary Windowpane* using the vocabulary words above, and continue to add vocabulary words throughout the unit. (RB p. 33)

KWL:

Begin the *KWL Chart* about Explorers and Missionaries. Once you have completed the unit, don't forget to add notes about what you learned in the final "L" column. (RB p. 35)

COMPILING DATA:

Fill in the *A to Z Chart* about Explorers and Missionaries as you proceed through this unit. (RB p. 21; example AG p. 106)

WRITING:

Research the Latin roots for the words *century, millennia,* and *decade*. What are some other words using the same roots? Calculate how many centuries and decades have passed since Columbus discovered the New World. (*Answer:* AG p. 107)

MATH:

A. Fill in the *Timeline* with important dates as you proceed through this unit. (RB p. 41)

B. Select and research three of the following boat sizes: canoe, paddle boat, sailboat, yacht, cruise ship (today's), Titanic, or Viking ships. Draw to scale your selected boats on graph paper.

SCIENCE:

To travel great distances over the sea, explorers needed dependable ships. Boat builders know that certain materials will float, and others will sink. Try this experiment: Fill a large container with water. Select at least ten different objects which will fit inside that container. First, make a prediction as to whether the object will sink or float. Then give it a try. Was your prediction correct? Why might you have two objects of the same size, and one sink and the other float? What properties of an object determine whether or not it will float?

GEOGRAPHY:

Identify the approximate coordinates (latitude and longitude) where Marco Polo started in Italy, three places he may have stopped along the way, and his final destination in China. What forms of travel did he use to get from one point to another? If you were to make that same journey today, what would be the most efficient way(s) to travel?

CRAFTS:

Make a Viking boat using milk or orange juice cartons (instructions can be easily found online). Be sure to decorate your ship, and test its ability to float and sail.

LOOK IT UP:

How many miles would you have to travel if you were to follow the equator and circumnavigate the Earth? (*Answer:* AG p. 103)

SPANISH EXPLORERS IN TEXAS

1. ***PINEDA*** (p. 54)
2. ***CABEZA DE VACA*** (pp. 55-56)
3. ***CORONADO*** (pp. 57-59)

VOCABULARY:

> ***parchment, reed, palmetto, resin, elements, viceroy, friar, trek, scribe, accurate, waterway,***
> ***barge, cultivated, prospect, crossbow, entourage, scout, mesa, truce, gorge, persist***

ECONOMICS:

> Estimate how much would it cost today to lease a vessel, hire a crew, and purchase supplies for a
> one-way, two-week journey by sea from Spain to Texas. How might that compare to the cost during
> the 1500s? Why might the cost be more or less?

WRITING:

> The explorers utilized their persuasive skills to convince monarchs to fund their expeditions.
> Write a persuasive argument requesting financial support for something you personally want or
> need.

COOKING:

> Try your hand at a typical 15th century Italian meal. Make ***Vermicelli!*** (AG p. 94)

GEOGRAPHY:

> One of Pineda's responsibilities was to create the first map of the Gulf Coast. Draw a map depicting
> the route from your home to the closest grocery store or other landmark, purely by walking. Be sure
> to include a compass rose and a map key.

CRAFTS:

> Add the Spanish flag to your ***Six Flags Activity Chart.*** (RB p. 39)

COMPILING DATA:

> Begin the ***Explorers Flip Book***. Cut along the large rectangle, fold in half, and cut through the
> dotted lines between each explorer's name. As you learn about each explorer, add facts about him
> and his voyage under each flap. (RB p. 64)

WHAT IF?:

> *What if* Cabeza de Vaca and his companions had never made it back to civilization? How might the
> absence of his reports regarding Texas have affected Spain's decision to continue exploration and
> colonization of the land?

LOOK IT UP:

> How many miles long is the Texas coastline? It can be measured in several ways. (*Answer:* AG p. 103)

FRENCH EXPLORERS IN TEXAS

pp. 60-61

VOCABULARY:

> ***waned, seaport, export, proposal, allies, delta, palisade, squall, venture***

ECONOMICS:

> When a new product becomes successful, other individuals often "jump on the bandwagon."
> The Spaniards found success in their explorations, and shortly after, the French followed suit. What
> are three products invented in your lifetime which were quickly copied and produced by others?
> Look up the definitions of the words *copyright* and *patent*.

WRITING:

A jingle is a short, catchy tune, similar to those you hear on t.v. commercials.

Rewrite the story of La Salle's attempt to form a settlement and its (and his) demise to a jingle tune.

COOKING:

Go to your local "epicurean" market and taste test five or six different French cheeses. Research French recipes and choose one to try at home.

CRAFTS:

Add the French flag to your *Six Flags Activity Chart* page. (RB p. 39)

WHAT IF?:

What if La Salle's colony had succeeded? Would the French have continued more exploration and settlements in Texas? Would Spain have accepted this peacefully? How might our lives be different if the French had a greater effect on our culture?

LOOK IT UP:

The sunken ship La Belle was eventually excavated and recovered during the 1990s. Name three artifacts found within the ship.

OTHER IMPORTANT TEXAS EXPLORERS

p. 62

VOCABULARY:

province, Puritans

LOOK IT UP:

Find the names of ten cities, counties, or schools in Texas named after Spanish or French explorers.

WHAT IF?:

What if other countries had attempted to colonize Texas? Perhaps Asian countries? Or African countries? Why might these faraway countries have been interested in colonizing Texas? How might our country and state be different today?

ART?:

Using your *Comic Strip* template, illustrate the story of three explorers studied in this unit. (RB p. 37)

COMPILING DATA?:

Complete the *Early Explorers to the New World* timeline, filling in the appropriate explorers' names to match the given dates. (RB p. 65; *Answer*: AG p. 110)

MISSIONS AND PRESIDIOS

pp. 63-68

VOCABULARY:

mission, presidio, settlement, prosperous, baptized, converts, clergy, secular, parish, bishops, privatize, encroaching, cavalry, depot, anagram, cultivate, bastion

COMPILING DATA:

A. Trace the *Mission Doors* on heavy paper and cut out. Fold doors in towards the middle and decorate the outside of doors to look like old wood. Add brass-colored hinges and door knobs. On the inside left door, make notes about the missionaries. On inside right door, write about the people who lived in the missions, and in the center, write about the layout of a typical mission. (RB p. 67)

B. Fill in the *Missions, Presidios, and Early Towns Chart*. (RB p. 68)

MATH/ECONOMICS:

It is estimated that each person uses about 4.85 bushels of corn each year (remember, corn products include much more than just corn on the cob!). What is the approximate population of the world today? How many bushels of corn must be grown each year to meet the needs of the world population? What is the current average cost of a bushel of corn? (*Answer*: AG p. 107)

WRITING:

There has been a mysterious incident in the mission! The milk cow has disappeared. Write one paragraph about the incident from the perspectives of each of the following: a missionary, an Indian, and a soldier.

COOKING:

Make *Flour Tortillas* using the recipe provided. (AG p. 95)

ANAGRAMS:

An anagram is created by rearranging the letters in one word to form another word. Choose 4-5 early Texas cities and/or explorers and create an anagram using the letters in their names. You might want to use *Scrabble* or *Bananagram* tiles for this activity.

GEOGRAPHY:

Map the *Major Missions of Texas*. (RB p. 66; *Answer*: AG p. 107)

CRAFT:

A. Construct a presidio out of legos.

B. Use the *Comic Strip* template to tell the story of a typical mission. (RB p. 37)

MATH:

Create a bar graph that represents the number of each size and/or color of legos used in your presidio project. Determine your presidio's area and perimeter.

LOOK IT UP:

A. What year was the Alamo's scalloped roofline completed? Hint: it was after the Battle of the Alamo.

B. The word "presidio" comes from the Latin word, "praesidium." What is a praesidium?

(*Answers to both #1 and #2*: AG p. 103)

UNIT TEST:

Complete the *Explorers and Missionaries Unit Test*. (RB p. 122-23; *Answers*: AG p. 101)

SUGGESTED READING:

Explorers in Early Texas by Betsy Warren

El Camino Real de los Tejas Map: https://www.nps.gov/elte/planyourvisit/brochures.htm

Legends of Texas: Volume 2, Pirates' Gold and Other Tales, edited by J. Frank Dobie

Let's Remember When Texas Belonged to Spain by Betsy Warren

The Missions of San Antonio by Mary Ann Noonan Guerra

Six Missions of Texas by Dorman H. Winfrey (historical coordinator)

Texas Missions: The Alamo and Other Texas Missions to Remember by Nancy Haston Foster

The Account (Relación) by Álvar Núñez Cabeza de Vaca [annotated translation] (teens and adults)

MOVIES and DOCUMENTARIES:
Spanish Texas DVD – Houston Arts and Media

ART TO EXPLORE:

Christopher Columbus by Sebastiano del Piombo
Coronado Sets Out to the North by Frederic Remington
Paintings of Cabeza de Vaca by Ted De Grazia
Paintings and Drawings of Cabeza de Vaca by Jose Cisneros
The Destruction of Mission San Saba by Jose de Paez
The Alamo watercolor by Mary Ann Adams Maverick (1838)

WRITING
PROMPT
PAGE 119

WEBSITES:

Conquistadors: www.thestoryoftexas.com/discover/campfire-stories/conquistadors
Mission System: https://tshaonline.org/handbook/online/articles/its02
Texas Missions: http://www.texasmissionguide.com/
The Alamo: http://www.thealamo.org/remember/history/chronology/index.html
Early Texas Exploration: http://texasindependencetrail.com/node/23797
El Camino Real: http://www.elcaminorealdelostejas.org/ (you'll find maps, lesson plans, and more about El Camino Real on this site)
Primary Source Documents For This Period: https://tshaonline.org/lone-star-history-links/1060
La Salle and Hispanic Texans History: http://texastimetravel.com/get-guides
Explorers: http://ageofex.marinersmuseum.org/index.php?page=theexplorers

MUSIC:

You can find beautiful Spanish and French music of the Renaissance online. Relax and listen to the melodic sounds of the lute, guitar, and other instruments of the time as you paint or draw a landscape the French and Spanish explorers may have encountered in Texas.

Music of the Alamo Book and CD by William R. Chemerka

Twenty Questions and Memory Game Suggestions:

Cabeza de Vaca, Coronado, Pineda, La Salle, Columbus, Esteban, Luis de Moscoso Alvarado, Alonso De León, Father Damian Massanet, Father Antonio de San Buenaventura y Olivares, Louis Saint-Denis, Juan de Oñate, conquistador, mission, Cortés, friar, La Belle ship

IT'S ABOUT TIME! Game Suggestions:

Pineda maps Gulf Coast (1519), Columbus "discovers" the Americas (1492), Coronado searches for Cities of Gold (1540), Cabeza de Vaca shipwrecked (1528), La Salle creates settlement (1684), Mission Ysleta founded (1682), East Texas Missions begin (1690), Mission San Antonio de Valero and Presidio San Antonio de Béxar are founded (1718), San Antonio becomes capital city of Texas (1772), Last mission in Texas, Nuestra Señora del Refugio, is built (1793)

PLACES TO VISIT:

San Antonio Missions National Historical Park (visit all five missions) – San Antonio
Presidio La Bahía - Goliad
Mission Nuestra Señora de los Dolores – San Augustine
Mission Espiritu Santo State Historic Site – Goliad
Mission Tejas State Park - Grapeland
Ysleta Mission and Socorro Mission - El Paso
San Elizario Presidio Chapel – El Paso
La Petit Belle – Palacios
La Belle Exhibit/Bob Bullock Museum - Austin
Travel the El Camino Real de los Tejas: Order the National Park Service pamphlet which provides a map of the El Camino Real Trail(s) through Mexico, Texas, and Louisiana.
https://www.nps.gov/elte/planyourvisit/brochures.htm

SUPPLY LIST:
- container filled with water
- objects for sink/float experiment
- milk or orange juice carton
- ingredients to make *Vermicelli*
- heavy brown paper for *Mission Doors*
- recipe ingredients for *Flour Tortillas*
- legos

FILIBUSTERS

p. 69

VOCABULARY:

outpost, province, ayuntamiento, alcalde, mestizo, Tejano, strife, filibuster, interior, neglect

VOCABULARY WINDOWPANE:

Complete the *Vocabulary Windowpane* using the vocabulary words above, and continue to add vocabulary words throughout the unit. (RB p. 33)

KWL:

Begin the *KWL Chart* on Filibusters and Empresarios. Once you have completed the unit, don't forget to add notes about what you learned in the final "L" column. (RB p. 35)

COMPILING DATA:

Fill in the Filibusters and Empresarios *A to Z Chart* as you proceed through this unit. (RB p. 21)

MATH:

Timeline: Fill in the timeline with important dates as you proceed through this unit. (RB p. 41)

Philip Nolan Expedition

p. 70

VOCABULARY:

wrangled, piracy, garrisons, confiscated, decreed

ART:

A. Use the *Comic Strip* template to illustrate this filibuster story. (RB p. 37)

B. Create a shoebox diorama of this filibuster story.

Gutierrez-Magee Expedition

pp. 70-71

VOCABULARY:

garner, republican, recruits

ART:

A. Use the *Comic Strip* template to illustrate this filibuster story. (RB p. 37)

James Long Expedition

pp. 71-72

VOCABULARY:

exiled, wrest

ART:

Use the *Comic Strip* template to illustrate this filibuster story. (RB p. 37)

Drama:

Involve friends and family members and act out this filibuster story. If an extra person is available, ask them to video your dramatic interpretation.

Jane Long

p. 72

Vocabulary:

petticoat, hammock

Writing:

Compare a land filibuster with a congressional filibuster. How are they similar? Different?

Copy Work:

A British poet named Lord Byron wrote a popular poem in 1814 called "The Corsair." Americans liked to believe the pirate in the poem was based on the notorious character Jean Lafitte. Copy these first lines from "The Corsair" and illustrate. Think PIRATES as you read it! Although this poem is long and more appropriate for older teens and adults, you might want to read more about the real-life story of pirate Lafitte—it is fascinating! (AG p. 98)

What If?:

What if one of these filibusters had been successful? Do you think Texas would have become a separate country indefinitely or would the United States have annexed Texas earlier?

Look It Up:

The pirate Lafitte brothers were mentioned in the previous section about James Long. Find out how Jean Lafitte met and worked with Jim Bowie, years before the Battle of the Alamo. This story reminds us how people who make poor choices can redeem their lives, as many settlers did after arriving in Texas. (*Answer*: AG p. 103)

MEXICO OVERTHROWS THE SPANISH EMPIRE

p. 72

Vocabulary:

royalists, social change, Catholicism

Compiling Data:

Add the Mexican flag to your *Six Flags Activity Chart.* (RB p. 39)

Copy Work:

Although we call it the *Mexican Constitution of 1824,* of course the people of Mexico would have used the Spanish name. First, copy the proper and complete name of this particular constitution in English, and then rewrite the name of the constitution in Spanish. (AG p. 98)

What If?:

What if Mexico had not overthrown the Spanish Empire? Would Texans still have led a revolution to independence? Could Texas have won independence if the revolution had been fought against Spain instead of Mexico?

Look It Up:

In the Mexican Constitution of 1824, what was the supreme executive power of the country called? *Hint: look up Article 74 of the Constitution of 1824.* (*Answer*: AG p. 103)

Cooking:

Try your hand at making the traditional Mexican food, *Frijoles* (beans). (AG p. 93)

Moses Austin

p. 73

VOCABULARY:

depression, empresario, land grant, league, labor

COMPILING DATA:

Complete the *Texas Empresario Chart*. (RB p. 69)

SCIENCE:

Compare climates of the colonists' homelands to what they experienced upon arriving in Texas. Why was the idea of moving appealing to these immigrants?

LOOK IT UP:

If Moses Austin had not run into an old friend on the street in San Antonio, the entire history of Texas might have been different. What was the name of that old friend? (*Answer*: AG p. 103)

WHAT IF?:

In light of the prior *Look It Up* question, what *would* have happened if Moses Austin had not run into that old friend in San Antonio? How might Texas history be different?

MATH:

Moses Austin used true horsepower to travel from Herculaneum, Missouri, to San Antonio, Texas. If you were to travel that same distance today by car, how many gallons of gas would it take and how many hours to travel the same approximate distance? (*Answer*: AG p. 107)

Stephen F. Austin

pp. 73-74

VOCABULARY:

idlers, militia, entice

MATH:

The immigrants could only bring what would fit in a covered wagon. If you were allowed only a 4x4 foot container, which when filled, could weigh no more than 100 pounds, what would you bring on your move?

CRAFT:

Design a poster Stephen F. Austin would have hung in the public square, advertising his search for 300 colonists to join him in moving to Texas.

WRITING:

The immigrants were expected to follow pre-agreed upon rules. Write seven rules you think should be applied to immigrants today.

COPY WORK:

Mary Austin Holley, cousin to Stephen F. Austin, moved to Texas in 1831. She wrote several books about Texas, including one that gave this description of the land. Perhaps the beauty of her words enticed Americans to make their new home in Texas. Copy her writing, then illustrate. (AG p. 98)

LOOK IT UP:

Did Stephen F. Austin ever marry and have children? (*Answer*: AG p. 103)

pp. 74-75

VOCABULARY:

infamous, squabbles

WRITING:

Pretend you are an immigrant who has been living in Texas for five years during this time period. Write a letter to someone who still lives in your home country, encouraging them to join you. Be sure to explain the benefits and what you have learned since your arrival in Texas.

COOKING:

Buttermilk Pie is a deliciously sweet pie that is said to have its roots in Britain, but made its way to Texas with the early settlers. Give it a try—you'll love it! (AG p. 95)

CRAFT:

Construct a log cabin out of your favorite art materials (clay, legos, popsicle sticks, balsa wood, recycled materials, etc.).

GEOGRAPHY:

Complete the *Texas Settlement Map Activity* (RB p. 70; use Texas map RB p. 9)

COPY WORK:

Pick one of the empresarios and copy the boundaries provided for their land grant.

http://www.tamu.edu/faculty/ccbn/dewitt/empresarios.htm#milam

MATH:

How many acres are in a league? How many acres are in a labor? How many square feet are in an acre? (*Answer*: AG p. 107)

LOOK IT UP:

Ben Milam became a well-known figure during the Texas Revolution, but he was also an empresario. Even more interesting, he was involved in not one, but two land grants. Where were they? (*Answer*: AG p. 103)

UNIT TEST:

Complete the *Filibusters and Empresarios Unit Test.* (RB p. 124-25; *Answers*: AG p. 101)

ART TO EXPLORE:

The Settlement of Austin's Colony by Henry McArdle
Stephen F. Austin by Louis Eyth
Jean Lafitte by R. Telfer
Jean Lafitte by E.H. Suydam
Father Hidalgo by Jose Clemente Orozco

SUGGESTED READING:

A Paradise Called Texas (trilogy) by Janice Jordan Shefelman
Johnny Texas by Carol Hoff (historical fiction)
Johnny Texas and the Old San Antonio Road by Carol Hoff (historical fiction)
Powderhorn Passage by Tom Townsend (historical fiction)
Pioneer Pups by Nancy Arnold (historical fiction)
Texas by Mary Austin Holley, written in 1831 (recent printing available - Austin: TSHA, 1990). [teens/adults]
Legends of Texas: Pirates Gold and Other Tales by J. Frank Dobie (teens and adults)

MOVIES AND DOCUMENTARIES:

Watch **Mr. Smith Goes to Washington**: After you read about the Texas filibusters, you might be interested in learning more about this term as used in a different setting. A filibuster can also refer to a different kind of "pirate" — not one who pirates or robs land—but one who pirates and takes over a debate. Occasionally in the Senate, a filibuster can be used to shut down debate and discussion of a bill in order to delay or prevent a vote. This old movie shows you how that is accomplished!

WEBSITES:

List of Early German Pioneers and Settlers in Texas:
tshaonline.org/handbook/online/browse/what/peoples/germans/biographies/pioneers-and-early-settlers
San Felipe de Austin site: http://www.visitsanfelipedeaustin.com/index.aspx?poage=17

MUSIC AND SONGS:

During the 1820s, an American dramatist named John Howard Payne wrote the lyrics to a song (melody by Sir Henry Bishop) called "Home! Sweet Home!" Find a recording of this piece online—you are sure to recognize the tune.

Mary Austin Holly, Stephen's cousin, moved to Texas during the early years of empresarios and wrote a song called "Brazos Boat Song." See if you can find it online!

Twenty Questions and Memory Game Suggestions:

Moses Austin, Stephen F. Austin, Jane Long, James Long, Philip Nolan, Gutiérrez de Lara, Jean Lafitte, Augustus Magee, Father Hidalgo, Hayden Edwards, Benjamin Edwards, Colonel José Joaquín de Arredondo, Martin De León

IT'S ABOUT TIME! Game Suggestions:

Philip Nolan Expedition (1800-1801), Gutiérrez-Magee Expedition (1812-1813), James Long Expedition (1819-1822), Mexico overthrows Spanish Empire (1821), Moses Austin visits Texas (1820), Stephen F. Austin begins to bring in settlers to his colony (1821), San Antonio becomes capital of the province (1772), Texas joins with Coahuila to form a state (1824), Fredonian Rebellion (1826)

PLACES TO VISIT:

Frontier Times Museum – Bandera
Spanish Governor's Palace – San Antonio
La Nina Replica Ship – Corpus Christi
Institute of Texan Cultures – San Antonio
Pioneer Village – Gonzales
Historic Grist Mill and Alsatian Homes – Castroville
Deaf Smith County Museum - Hereford
1877 Tall Ship Elissa – Galveston
San Felipe de Austin State Historic Site - San Felipe

WRITING
PROMPT
PAGE 121

SUPPLY LIST:

- posterboard
- building materials for log cabin model construction
- ingredients for *Buttermilk Pie*

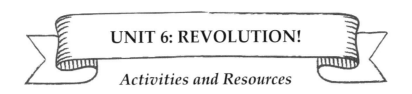

UNIT 6: REVOLUTION!

Activities and Resources

⊣ TERÁN AND THE LAW OF APRIL 6, 1830 ⊢

p. 77

VOCABULARY:

reign, centralized, halted, suspended, custom duties, immigration

VOCABULARY WINDOWPANE:

Complete the *Vocabulary Windowpane* using the vocabulary words above, and continue to add vocabulary words throughout the unit. (RB p. 33)

KWL:

Begin the *KWL Chart* on the Texas Revolution. Once you have completed the unit, don't forget to add notes about what you learned in the final "L" column. (RB p. 35)

COMPILING DATA:

Fill in the *A to Z Chart* about the Texas Revolution as you proceed through this unit. (RB p. 21)

MATH:

Timeline: Fill in important dates on the timeline as you proceed through this unit. (RB p. 41)

GEOGRAPHY:

Using a large Texas map (we recommend drawing a large map on a cheap white shower curtain), label the major rivers and towns. Then, as you read through this unit, use a set of characters (see supply list below for directions) and move those characters across the map as you learn about them and the locations where they played an important role.

GAME:

Play the teacher-led *Changing the Rules Game.* (RB p. 71)

WHAT IF?:

As you continue to read through the *Revolution* unit, think how history might have changed if Terán had not presented information leading to the Law of April 6, 1830.

COPY WORK:

Copy interesting excerpts from Terán's report or recommendations, as well as Article 9 from the April 6, 1830 Decree: **http://www.tamu.edu/faculty/ccbn/dewitt/consultations1.htm**

⊣ TROUBLE AT ANAHUAC ⊢

p. 78

VOCABULARY:

merchant, harboring, rile, martial law, skirmish, federalism, hindsight

SCIENCE:

Travis was unable to escape without help. Often one event impacts and leads to another. Just for fun, watch some Rube Goldberg videos about chain reactions. Create your own Rube Goldberg design with a ball named "Travis" and help him find a way to escape from his imprisonment.

GAME:

Play the teacher-led *Growing Unrest Simulation.* (RB pp. 72-73)

ECONOMICS:

What were the top ten occupations of Americans during the 1830s? What are the top ten American occupations today?

LOOK IT UP:

From where does the city of *Anahuac* get its unusual name? (*Answer*: AG p. 104)

BATTLE OF VELASCO

p. 78

VOCABULARY:

manned

LOOK IT UP:

What is the present-day name of the town then known as Velasco? (*Answer*: AG p. 104)

BATTLE OF NACOGDOCHES

pp. 78-79

VOCABULARY:

arms, discharged, evacuation, cuartel

COPY WORK:

Copy a firsthand account written by a real survivor of the Texas Revolution and illustrate. Here is one source you might like to use:

https://texasalmanac.com/sites/default/files/images/Survivors1872b.pdf

ART:

Use the *Comic Strip* template to tell the continuing saga of Anahuac, Velasco, and the Battle of Nacogdoches. (RB p. 37)

SANTA ANNA

p. 79

VOCABULARY:

high station, criollo, cadet, infantry, ruthless, cited, democracy, centralist, dictator, disbanded

WHAT IF?:

What if Santa Anna had been kind and benevolent, instead of the ruthless leader he would become over time? Would Texas have still decided to declare independence?

LOOK IT UP:

Santa Anna remained an interesting character, even after the Texas Revolution. In fact, many years before he actually died, he held a funeral for one of his body parts! Do a little research and see if you can find out what he "lost," and how he made sure his countrymen honored him (or, a part of him, that is!). (*Answer*: AG p. 104)

CONVENTIONS OF 1832 AND 1833

p. 80

VOCABULARY:

limited, levy, resolutions, exempt, tyranny, startling, mentor

WRITING:

Write a two-paragraph essay on how to determine when change needs to happen.

MATH:

An important grievance expressed by Texans concerned the great distance to travel and communicate with the central government. At that time, the state government capital was located in Saltillo, and later Monclova, Coahuila; Mexico's capital was located in Mexico City.

Calculate how many miles one would have to travel between San Felipe and each of these cities. Then calculate the distance between San Felipe, the current state capital of Austin, and our country's capital of Washington, D.C. (*Answer*: AG p. 107)

COPY WORK:

You'll find a copy of the treatises presented to Mexico, resulting from the Convention of 1833, published in the book ***The History of Texas*** (1836) by David B. Edward. Copy all or part of the paragraph that relates to the issues caused by living at such a great distance from the state capital. (AG p. 98)

AUSTIN'S TRIP TO MEXICO

p. 81

VOCABULARY:

authorities, grant, reforms, conceded

WRITING:

Write a letter from Stephen F. Austin to *Dear Abby* (if you don't know who that is, ask your teacher/ mom), looking for advice as he sits in jail, and then compose Abby's response.

WHAT IF?:

What if Stephen F. Austin had **not** been imprisoned? *What if* Mexico had agreed to the Texans' requests?

SCIENCE:

Make a list of at least five words for each of your five senses to describe Austin's jail cell.

LOOK IT UP:

When Austin was imprisoned in Mexico City, he was initially only allowed a few visitors. One was his lawyer, and the other was able to bring Austin reading materials. Who was that man? (AG p. 104)

TROUBLE CONTINUES . . .

p. 81

VOCABULARY:

disloyal, quash

WRITING:

Create baseball-style trading cards for these four major "players": Moses Austin, Stephen F. Austin, General Terán, and Santa Anna. Be sure to include their vital statistics along with their key strengths and weaknesses.

COPY WORK:

While in prison, Stephen F. Austin wrote in a journal. Copy this prison diary entry from February 22, 1834, and illustrate. (AG p. 98)

ART:

Use the ***Comic Strip*** template and tell the story of the Conventions in San Felipe and Austin's trip to Mexico. (RB p. 37)

p. 82

VOCABULARY:

Texians, self-government, reinforcements, emblazoned, embroidered

WRITING:

Write an informative article for the Gonzales newspaper regarding the Battle of Gonzales. Be sure to include only facts. Don't forget the five w's and h: *who, what, when, where, why, and how.*

MATH:

Determine the ratio of Texians to Mexicans during the Battle of Gonzales. (*Answer:* AG p. 107)

SCIENCE:

Legend has it when there were no more cannon balls to be used, the Texians instead shot scrap metal, chains, horseshoes, etc. out of the mouth of the cannon. You can find many ideas for building a catapult online or in your library. Build your own catapult and gather six items which can be shot from your catapult. Predict which will fly the farthest. Test your predictions and record your results.

COMPILING DATA:

A. Begin adding information for each of the *Battles of the Texas Revolution* as you study them. (RB pp. 74-75)

B. Fill in important events on the *Revolution Calendars*, beginning with the Battle of Gonzales. Continue with each new battle or event. (RB pp. 76-85)

WHAT IF?:

What if Castañeda and his soldados had captured the Gonzales cannon? How might the loss of the cannon have affected the Texans' morale? Would they have been discouraged, or even more dedicated to winning Texas independence?

LOOK IT UP:

Castañeda moved his campsite upriver from the initial encampment, to a spot where he could cross "without embarrassment" . . . in other words, an area less defended by the Texans. Who owned the land where the Mexican Army set up their second camp? (*Answer*: AG p. 104)

ART:

Use your *Comic Strip* template to tell the story of the Battle of Gonzales. (RB p. 37)

MARCH TO GOLIAD AND SAN ANTONIO

pp. 82-83

VOCABULARY:

supply line, military siege, blockade, caravan, payroll

WRITING:

A. Create a *Comic Strip* summarizing the Grass Fight. (RB p. 37)

B. Write a 1-2 page movie or play script depicting the events of the Grass Fight.

COMPILING DATA:

Continue filling in your *Revolution Calendar* and *Battle Charts.* (RB pp. 74-75, 76-85)

SCIENCE:

What weighs more—a pound of grass or a pound of gold? Which has the greater volume? Which has the greater density? (*Answer*: AG p. 107)

CRAFT:

Take a break and pick some weeds! Use the native grasses in your area to paint a picture with the grass blades. Observe the differences in shape, form, and texture.

LOOK IT UP:

What is the distance between Mission Concepción and the Alamo? (*Answer*: AG p. 104)

p. 83

VOCABULARY:

tragic, discouraged

COPY WORK:

Look up and copy a paragraph from Stephen F. Austin's March 7th address delivered to Louisville, Kentucky, pleading for support and explaining the Texas cause for revolt.

http://www.pbs.org/weta/thewest/resources/archives/two/txaustin.htm

LOOK IT UP:

Near what famous house was Ben Milam shot? Hint: Jim Bowie knew that house well. (AG p. 104)

http://www.tamu.edu/faculty/ccbn/dewitt/milamben.htm

COMPILING DATA:

Continue filling in your *Revolution Calendar* and *Battle Charts.*

WHAT IF?:

What if the Texians had not released Cos and his men? What would have happened if they had kept the soldados prisoner? Would that act affect the outcome at the Alamo a few months later?

CONSULTATION AT SAN FELIPE

p. 84

VOCABULARY:

aggressive, quest, provisional, commissioners, regular army, authority, imminent

COMPILING DATA:

Continue filling in your *Revolution Calendar*. (RB pp. 76-85)

ART:

Use your *Comic Strip* template and tell the story of the Texians fighting their way into San Antonio and the Consultation at San Felipe. (RB p. 37)

BACK IN SAN ANTONIO

pp. 84-85

VOCABULARY:

enlisted, renegades, traitors, abandon, reinforcements, private (soldier), courier, soldados

COPY WORK: *SPOILER ALERT!* (*If your student is not familiar with the outcome of the Battle of the Alamo, save this Copy Work and the following What If for the next section.*)

Copy part or all of Lieutenant Colonel William Barret Travis' plea for help in the letter he wrote February 24th, 1836. The letter is fairly short in length. Memorize and present this dramatic call for help to your fellow students and/or family. The letter is easily found with an online search.

WHAT IF?: *ANOTHER SPOILER ALERT!*

What if the Texian soldiers at the Alamo had surrendered to Santa Anna? Would they have still all lost their lives? Would their surrender inspire or discourage the other Texians who would later battle Santa Anna at San Jacinto?

COMPILING DATA:

Continue filling in your *Revolution Calendar*. (RB pp. 76-85)

pp. 86-87

VOCABULARY:

> *fortify, palisades, compound, refugees, barricaded, complex, bombardment, no quarter, Deguello, invoked*

WRITING:

> There are, and have been for many years, general rules of war. These rules were created to protect prisoners, non-participants, and the wounded. Compare the differences in the ways in which Santa Anna and the Texian leaders handled their victories throughout the Texas Revolution. Take it a step further and read the Geneva Convention's Rules of War in use today.

CRAFT:

> A. Sketch the Alamo complex and label the positions of known individual Texian fighters.
> B. Make a 3-D Alamo and draw scenes in each section. (RB p. 91)
> C. Tell the battle story using the *Comic Strip* template. (RB p. 37)

COMPILING DATA:

> Continue filling in your *Revolution Calendar* and *Battle Charts*. (RB pp. 74-75 and 76-85)

HANDS ON:

> Estimate the true value of 182 (number of Texian soldiers) and 2,000 (approximate number of Mexican soldados) by placing two different types or colors of beans in two separate piles. Count and see how close you were, and then add or subtract from your piles as you count the actual numbers. Sprinkle the 182 beans inside your rendition of the Alamo, and pour the 2,000 beans around the outside perimeter. Now do you see what the Texians were up against?

WHAT IF?

> *What if* Jim Bowie had followed General Houston's advice to destroy the Alamo. How might the rest of the Revolution have changed? How might our lives be different today? Or would they?

COMPILING DATA:

> Fill in the *Juan Seguín* chart. (RB p. 86; *Answers*: RG p. 107)

CONVENTION OF 1836

pp. 88-89

VOCABULARY:

> *dissolved, unanimously, draft, ad interim, vital, blue-norther, violation, petition, corrupt, delegates*

COMPILING DATA:

> Compare the United States and Texas Declarations of Independence and Constitutions. Find five similarities and five differences between the documents.

WRITING:

> Rewrite Travis' February 24th letter using language Americans today can understand.

COMPILING DATA:

> Continue filling in your *Revolution Calendar*. (RB pp. 76-85)

DISASTER IN GOLIAD

pp. 89-90

VOCABULARY:

> *mercy, massacre*

COMPILING DATA:

Continue filling in your *Revolution Calendar* and *Battle Charts*. (RB pp. 74-75 and 76-85)

WRITING:

Send a warning to Goliad and Colonel Fannin in twenty words or less.

WHAT IF?:

What if Fannin and his men had successfully traveled to San Antonio and reinforced the Alamo? Would there have been a sufficient number of additional Texan soldiers to have made a difference in the outcome?

CRAFT:

A. Listen to a symphonic dramatic piece, such as Chopin's "Funeral March." Paint as you listen, expressing the mood and emotion of the piece.

B. Tell the story of the Massacre at Goliad with your *Comic Strip* template. (RB p. 37)

COPY WORK:

Sam Houston sent a letter to Fannin, ordering him to move his troops to Victoria. Copy this order and draw a map that Houston intended Fannin to follow. You can find the order here:

http://www.tamu.edu/faculty/ccbn/dewitt/andrew3.htm#fannin%20letter

THE RUNAWAY SCRAPE

pp. 90-91

VOCABULARY:

slaughter, lure, Runaway Scrape, taunted, defy, drill

MATH:

Santa Anna divided his army into three groups (Gaona to the north, Urrea to the south, and Santa Anna through the center). Figure out the percentages of each group in relation to the total number of Santa Anna's troops. (*Answer:* AG p. 107)

GEOGRAPHY:

Approximately how many miles of travel were involved for Santa Anna's troops, marching from Béxar to San Jacinto? How many miles for Houston and the Texians, marching from Gonzales to San Jacinto? (*Answer:* AG p. 107)

WRITING:

Knowing they could not carry everything, many of the Texian refugees buried their valuable and prized possessions prior to leaving home. Make two lists: one with items you would bury and come back for later, and one with items you would carry with you.

CRAFT:

Using dark crayons to emphasize the muddy terrain, illustrate a scene from the Runaway Scrape with the crayon-resist method. (Use good pressure to create your picture with crayons, then a muddy-brown watercolor brushed over the surface of the picture. The crayon areas will resist the paint.)

HANDS ON:

Develop a list of questions to ask Sam Houston about his decision to wait and fight. Recreate the scene with a partner in the form of an interview. Videotape and critique your interview skills.

COPY WORK:

Copy a firsthand account of the Runaway Scrape, narrated by Creed Taylor (1900) in "Tall Men With Long Rifles," written by James T. DeShields. You'll find this account here:

http://www.tamu.edu/faculty/ccbn/dewitt/mustergon.htm

pp. 92-95

VOCABULARY:

capital, cutlass, siesta, convictions, ironic, persisted

COPY WORK:

Copy the first three articles from the public version of the *Treaty of Velasco*. (AG p. 99)

MATH:

The Battle of Jacinto lasted only eighteen minutes. Track and record how far you can walk, how many sentences you can write, and how many pages in a book you can read in eighteen minutes.

SCIENCE:

Tidal marshlands, as found at the San Jacinto battle site, are home to numerous diverse plants and animals. Research the marshland ecosystems, and list ten plants and animals typically found in this habitat.

WRITING:

If you were a refugee who had run away before San Jacinto, upon learning of the success of the Texian army, would you have returned to Texas? Why or why not? Write a paragraph explaining your stance.

WHAT IF?

A. *What if* Santa Anna had not divided his army into thirds, but instead sent all the troops to San Jacinto?

B. *What if* General Houston had listened to his angry soldiers and executed Santa Anna following the battle?

COMPILING DATA:

Continue filling in your *Revolution Calendar* and *Battle Charts*. (RB pp. 74-75 and 76-85)

CRAFT:

A. Create a **WANTED: DEAD OR ALIVE** poster advertising a reward for the return of the escaped leader of the Mexican Army.

B. Tell the story of the Battle of San Jacinto with your *Comic Strip* template. (RB p. 37)

VENN DIAGRAM:

Compare the similarities and differences between Santa Anna and Sam Houston using a *Venn Diagram*. If you find this topic interesting, older students and adults might enjoy reading James Michener's *The Eagle and the Raven*. (RB p. 23)

GAME:

Play *"I Have, Who Has" Texas Revolution*. (RB pp. 88-90; *Answers*: AG p. 108)

Cut out each of the rectangular cards, mix them up, and dole out evenly. The student with the card which says "I have Santa Anna" reads their card out loud first. Whoever has the answer to the bottom portion of the card, responds with "I have..." and then reads the bottom of their own card. Play continues until the the first person is able to respond with "I have Santa Anna."

If playing in a small group, dole out the cards evenly, again starting with the Santa Anna card. As each card is read, turn it upside down on the table. The first person to get rid of all their cards wins.

If playing alone and/or at home, this can be used as a study tool and set up like dominoes. The student can independently try to put all the cards in the correct order.

CAUSE AND EFFECT:

Fill out *Texas Revolution Cause and Effect Chart*. (RB p. 87)

UNIT TEST:

Complete the *Revolution Unit Test*. (RB pp. 126-27; *Answers*: AG p. 101)

SUGGESTED READING:

Magnificent Sam: The Amazing Adventures of Sam Houston by Laurie Cockerell

The Boy in the Alamo by Margaret Cousins (historical fiction)

Susanna of the Alamo by John Jakes

The Great Texas Scare: A Story of the Runaway Scrape by Martha Tannery Jones (historical fiction)

Race to Velasco by Paul N. Spellman (historical fiction)

General Houston's Little Spy by Cara Skinner (historical fiction)

Texas: Cowboys and Campfires by Nancy Alana

THC Texas Independence Trail Map: http://texasindependencetrail.com/

Voices of the Alamo by Sherry Garland

Sam Houston: For Texas and the Union by Walter M. Woodward

Texas Tales Illustrated: The Revolution by Jack Patton and John Rosenfield

New Texas History Movies by Jack Jackson

Texas by Terán edited by Jack Jackson (teens/adults)

ART TO EXPLORE:

The Battle of San Jacinto by Henry Arthur McArdle

Antonio López de Santa Anna by Carlos Paris

Deaf Smith by T. Jefferson Wright

Surrender of Santa Anna by William Henry Huddle

William Barret Travis by Henry Arthur McArdle

Dawn at the Alamo by Henry Arthur McArdle

Davy Crockett by John Neagle

General Sam Houston at the Battle of San Jacinto by S. Seymour Thomas

The Fall of the Alamo by Robert Jenkins Onderdonk

Juan Seguín by Jefferson Wright

Three statues by Craig Campbella (see under *Places to Visit* section)

MOVIES/DOCUMENTARIES:

Sam Houston: American Statesman, Soldier, and Pioneer (2011)
D. Florian, Producer

Gone to Texas aka *Houston: The Legend of Texas* (1986) Republic Pictures

The Alamo (2004) Touchstone Pictures

Washington-on-the-Brazos: The Politics of Revolution (Houston Arts and Media)

San Antonio and the Alamo (Houston Arts and Media)

WEBSITES:

The Alamo: www.thealamo.org
San Jacinto: http://www.sanjacinto-museum.org/
Washington-on-the-Brazos: http://wheretexasbecametexas.org/
Texas Independence Trail Sites:
http://texasindependencetrail.com/plan-your-adventure/themes/main-texas-revolution
Texas Revolution and Sam Houston: samhoustonmovie.com
Treaties of Velasco: http://www.lsjunction.com/docs/velasco.htm
San Jacinto Personal Account:
http://www.tamu.edu/faculty/ccbn/dewitt/sanjacintotaylor.htm

WRITING
PROMPT
PAGE 123

Twenty Questions and Memory Game Suggestions:

William Barret Travis, Manuel de Mier y Terán, Santa Anna, Ben Milam, Juan Seguín, Deaf Smith, Sam Houston, Jim Bowie, General Martín Perfecto de Cos, James Fannin, David Burnet, Lorenzo de Zavala, Davy Crockett, Henry Smith, Susanna Dickinson, Colonel John Davis Bradburn, Colonel Domingo de Ugartechea, Colonel Piedras, Lieutenant Fransisco De Castañeda, Colonel James C. Neill, General José de Urrea, General Antonio Gaona, the Golden Standard, the Twin Sisters

IT'S ABOUT TIME! Game Suggestions:

Teran's report leads to Law of April 6 (1830), Travis imprisoned at Anahuac (1832), Austin travels to Mexico (1833), Battle of Gonzales (October 2,1835), Texians take Béxar and the Alamo from General Cos (December 1835), Battle of the Alamo (March 6, 1836), Declaration of Independence from Mexico and Constitution written (March 2, 1836), Massacre at Goliad (March 27, 1836), Battle of San Jacinto (April 21, 1836)

MUSIC:
"Will You Come to the Bower?"
music/song played at the Battle of San Jacinto
Fathers of Texas CD by KR Wood
"Ballad of the Alamo" by Marty Robbins
"El Deguello"

PLACES TO VISIT:

The Alamo (Mission San Antonio de Valero) – San Antonio
San Jacinto Battleground State Historic Site – La Porte
Gonzales Memorial Museum – Gonzales
Presidio La Bahía - Goliad
Fannin Memorial Monument - Goliad
Fannin Battleground State Historic Site - Fannin
Goliad State Park and Mission Espiritu Santo de Zuniga State Historic Site - Goliad
Fort Anahuac Park - Anahuac
San Felipe de Austin State Historic Site – San Felipe
Washington-on-the-Brazos State Historic Site - Washington
Stroll Through Texas History - Acton (Texas Heroes Foundation)
Lady Liberty Statue/Spirit of Texas Eternal Flame - Conroe (Spirit of Texas Bank)
Lone Star Monument and Historical Flag Park ("The Texian" statue) - Conroe
José Antonio Navarro and Stephen F. Austin Statue - The Woodlands

Three statues sculpted by Craig Campobella:

- **Lady Liberty Statue**, as seen on the San Jacinto Battle Flag (Taysha Park/The Spirit of Texas Bank, Conroe). Within the base of the *Lady Liberty Statue* you can view the **Spirit of Texas Eternal Flame**, lit by Sam Houston IV in 2015.
- **José Antonio Navarro and Stephen F. Austin** (The Woodlands: Lake Front Circle and Six Pines Drive)
- **The Texian** (Lone Star Flag Park, Conroe)

Photographs courtesy of Denton Florian.

SUPPLY LIST:

- inexpensive white shower curtain
- two bags of different colored beans
- materials to make a catapult and "ammo" for your catapult
- paint and various sizes and shapes of weeds/grass
- crayons and paint for crayon-resist activity
- small plastic soldiers labeled as historical figures of the Texas Revolution. You might want to use different colors for the Texian soldiers and the Mexican soldados so you can easily distinguish which "side" they represent.

A NEW COUNTRY BEGINS

pp. 97-98

VOCABULARY:

officials, congress, capitol, azure

VOCABULARY WINDOWPANE:

Complete the *Vocabulary Windowpane* using the vocabulary words above, and continue to add vocabulary words throughout the unit. (RB p. 33)

KWL:

Begin the *KWL Chart* regarding the Republic of Texas. Once you have completed the unit, don't forget to add notes about what you learned in the final "L" column. (RB p. 35)

MATH:

Timeline: Fill in important dates on the timeline as you proceed through this unit. (RB p. 41)

COMPILING DATA:

A. Fill in the *A to Z Chart* about the Republic of Texas as you proceed through this unit. (RB p. 21)

B. Add the Lone Star flag to your *Six Flags Activity Chart.* (RB p. 39)

WRITING:

The new republic knew one of their first responsibilities would be to pay off their debt. Devise a creative way to raise money in the 1800s.

LOOK IT UP:

Approximately what was the debt the Republic owed after the Texas Revolution (accumulated by the provisional and ad interim governments)? What is the current national debt of the United States? How much more debt does the United States owe at this time than the Republic of Texas owed after the Revolution? (*Answer*: AG p. 104)

FIRST THINGS FIRST: SAM HOUSTON, FIRST PRESIDENT OF THE REPUBLIC OF TEXAS

pp. 98-99

VOCABULARY:

annexation, reject, recognition, negotiate, furloughed, credit, tariffs, imported, enacted

WRITING:

Most Texans were happy to be free of Mexico's control, but some had hoped Texas would eventually be annexed and become one of the United States. On the other hand, some Texans hoped to remain an independent republic. Think about the reasons both held their opinions, and complete the *Should Texas Be Annexed to the U.S.?* activity. (RB p. 93)

CRAFT:

Pretend the new Texas government has selected you to design the front of the new dollar bill. What will you include and why? Illustrate.

LOOK IT UP:

Sam Houston's first "executive mansion" in Houston was located at what is now the corner of Main and Preston in the downtown area. What well-known national fast food restaurant is located where President Houston once lived? (*Answer*: AG p. 104)

Math:

What was the ratio of slave versus free states in 1837? (*Answer:* AG p. 108)

Copy Work:

Copy the names of the gentlemen who served as Houston's first cabinet:
https://www.tsl.texas.gov/exhibits/presidents/houston2/mrprez.html

Writing/performance:

Either write your own play, or perform the "Republic of Texas" short play from the book ***Texas History Classroom Plays***. Be sure to educate your audience about the personalities and issues of this important time in Texas history. (See the following *Suggested Reading* for this wonderful resource.)

MIRABEAU LAMAR: THE REPUBLIC'S SECOND PRESIDENT

pp. 99-100

Vocabulary:

consecutive, claim, tribal representatives, archives, restoration, debt, populace

Writing:

Choose three state and/or national issues in the news today. How would Houston and Lamar have reacted to these issues? Write a short speech from their perspectives.

Geography:

Properties for two universities were set aside during this period. Using the Texas map (RB p. 9), indicate the location of ten universities or colleges in Texas, including their names and the dates they were established.

Math:

Set up a budget for a new republic. Remember to include building projects, salaries, military expenses, etc.

Look It Up:

Who served as Mirabeau Lamar's Vice President of the Republic of Texas? (*Answer:* AG p. 104)

Copy Work:

Sam Houston and Mirabeau Lamar disagreed on many different topics. Unhappy that Lamar would follow him as President of the Republic, Sam Houston made sure his appearance at Lamar's inauguration would be unforgettable. Sam donned a powdered white wig, dressed much like George Washington, and gave a three-hour farewell speech before the new President Lamar even had a chance to speak himself. By the time Sam's speech was over, Lamar was so upset he could not speak at all. An eyewitness related the story. Copy this excerpt from his account and then illustrate this funny story in Texas history. (AG p. 99)

THE SANTA FE EXPEDITION

p. 100

Vocabulary:

expedition, intense

Copy Work:

In an address written to the people of Santa Fe in 1841, Lamar noted reasons they might want to join Texas and the freedom it would provide. Copy this brief section of the address. (AG p. 99)

Writing:

Think about Lamar's description of life in the Republic of Texas. Consider our lives today. Do you believe we live under the same freedoms Texans possessed in 1841? Write a persuasive letter to invite a friend to come live in Texas because of the freedoms it offers.

WHAT IF?:

Mirabeau Lamar was an interesting man. He was brave in battle, worked hard to make education a priority in Texas, and yet at the same time, worked just as hard to rid Texas of Native Americans— many of whom lived their lives quietly and innocently. What if Lamar had *not* been elected president of the Republic of Texas? How might Texas be different today?

PRESIDENT SAM HOUSTON'S SECOND TERM

pp. 100-101

VOCABULARY:

feud, occupation (of land)

WRITING:

Complete the *T-Chart* comparing Houston and Lamar as presidents of the Republic of Texas, then pull these ideas together into a three paragraph essay. Complete the essay by stating your opinion regarding whether Houston or Lamar was the more effective president. Provide evidence to support your opinion. (RB p. 92; *Answer*: AG p. 111)

ART:

Read the short Sam Houston biography, ***Magnificent Sam: The Amazing Adventures of Sam Houston***, together. When you reach the page where Sam receives his "Honor" ring, stop what you are doing. Take a few minutes to draw a similar ring on a yellow or gold sheet of paper. Decorate the ring with pictures of people doing things that are honorable. As you complete the book, hold on to your "ring." Whenever Sam Houston shows honor, raise your ring and say "Honor!" Do you think the ring on Sam's finger helped him remember to do what is right and honorable?

LOOK IT UP:

Sam Houston married during the span of time between his first and second terms as president. His "first lady" was a beautiful woman from Alabama. What was her name, and how many children did the two have together? (*Answer*: AG p. 104)

THE MIER EXPEDITION

pp. 101-102

VOCABULARY:

patrol

MATH:

What was the ratio of men who selected black beans to men who selected white beans?
What was the ratio of men who selected black beans to the total number of prisoners?
What was the ratio of men who selected white beans to the total number of prisoners?
If 17 prisoners were executed, how many prisoners were spared?
(*Answer*: AG p. 108)

LOOK IT UP:

How did some of the Mier Expedition prisoners escape Perote prison? (*Answer*: AG p. 104)

ANSON JONES:
LAST PRESIDENT OF THE REPUBLIC OF TEXAS

p. 102

WHAT IF:

What if the United States or Texas had decided *against* annexation? How would that have changed the future of the United States and of the Republic of Texas? Do you believe Texas would have eventually been annexed at a later date?

CRAFT:

Choose your favorite Republic of Texas President: Lamar, Houston, or Jones. Design a campaign flier for your candidate.

ART:

A. Using the **Comic Strip** template, tell the story of the three presidents of the republic. Address both problems and successes. (RB p. 37)

B. Draw caricatures of the faces of all three presidents of the Republic of Texas.

UNIT TEST:

Complete the **Republic of Texas Unit Test.** (RB pp. 128-29; *Answers:* RG pp. 102)

SUGGESTED READING:

Texas History Classroom Plays by Fred Cooper (www.singnlearn.com)
The Paper Republic by James P. Bevill (teens/adults)
Let's Remember When Texas Was a Republic by Betsy Warren
Daily Life in the Republic of Texas by Joseph William Schmitz
Log Cabin Cooking by Barbara Swell

ART TO EXPLORE:

General Sam Houston by Martin Johnson Heade
Mirabeau B. Lamar by William H. Huddle
Anson Jones by William H. Huddle
Andrew Jackson by Thomas Sully
Black Bean Episode by Frederic Remington
Angelina Eberly statue by Pat Oliphant

WEBSITES:

Independence Trail Republic of Texas Sites:
http://texasindependencetrail.com/plan-your-adventure/themes/main-republic-texas
Republic of Texas Currency:
https://www.tsl.texas.gov/treasures/republic/currency-01.html
Constitution of the Republic:
https://tarltonapps.law.utexas.edu/constitutions/texas1836

Twenty Questions and Memory Game Suggestions:

Sam Houston, Mirabeau Lamar, Anson Jones, Adrián Woll,
Colonel William S. Fisher, Angelina Eberly, President Andrew Jackson, Stephen F. Austin,
Chief Bowles, General Alexander Somervell, Felix Huston, Cynthia Ann Parker,
Santa Fe Expedition, Mier Expedition, Archives War

WRITING
PROMPT
PAGE 125

IT'S ABOUT TIME Game Suggestions:

Sam Houston elected first President of the Republic of Texas (September, 1836), Mirabeau Lamar elected President of the Republic of Texas (1838), Lamar moves archives and capital to Waterloo/Austin (1839), Santa Fe Expedition (1841), Sam Houston's second term as President of the Republic of Texas begins (1841), Adrián Woll and Mexican Army occupy San Antonio for a short time (September, 1842), Mier Expedition (December, 1842), Black Bean Episode (March, 1843), Anson Jones elected President of the Republic of Texas (1844), Lamar orders removal of Cherokees (1839)

PLACES TO VISIT:

Replica of First Texas Capitol – West Columbia
Stephen F. Austin Gravesite – Austin (Texas State Cemetery)
The Republic of Texas Museum – Austin
Star of the Republic Museum - Washington
Barrington Living History Farm (Anson Jones' farm) – Washington
Columbia Historical Museum – West Columbia
Independence Baptist Church – Independence
Washington-on-the-Brazos State Historic Site – Washington
Angelina Eberly Statue – Austin (6th and Congress, downtown)
Frontier Texas Museum - Abilene
Monument Hill State Historic Site - La Grange

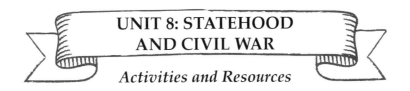

TEXAS JOINS THE UNITED STATES OF AMERICA

pp. 103-104

VOCABULARY:

rejected, enthusiastic, wary, majority, acquiring, expansion, joint resolution, simple majority, public lands, ratified, consented, resolution, Stars and Stripes, Manifest Destiny

VOCABULARY WINDOWPANE:

Complete the *Vocabulary Windowpane* using the vocabulary words above, and continue to add vocabulary words throughout the unit. (RB p. 33)

KWL:

Begin the *KWL Chart* regarding Texas Statehood and the Civil War. Once you have completed the unit, don't forget to add notes about what you learned in the final "L" column. (RB p. 35)

COMPILING DATA:

Fill in the *A to Z Chart* about Statehood and the Civil War as you proceed through this unit. (RB p. 21)

WRITING:

Compare the powers of Texas as a republic and as a state. What powers were lost and/or gained as Texas transitioned to become one of the United States?

CRAFTS:

Add the United States flag to your *Six Flags Activity Chart*. (RB p. 39)

MATH:

A. *Timeline*: Fill important dates in the timeline as you proceed through this unit. (RB p. 41)
B. The Texas senators who represented Texas in Washington, D.C., had to travel many miles to the country's capital. How many miles would they have traveled between Austin and Washington, D.C.? How long would it take them to travel that far by horse? By train? How long would it take today by car or by airplane? (*Answers*: AG p. 108)

SCIENCE:

Research the most important inventions created during the 1860s.

WHAT IF:

What if those inventions had never been created? What would life be like without them?

LOOK IT UP:

A famous American national figure said, "Texas was the great scheme that occupied me." Who was it? (*Answer*: AG p. 104)

TEXAS: A NEW STATE AND NEW CITIZENS

pp. 104-105

VOCABULARY:

frontier, investing, barons, counties, House of Representatives, Senate, Supreme Court

COOKING:

Make some delicious *Peanut Brittle,* a popular treat in the late 1800s, for your family! (AG p. 96)

WRITING:

Write a letter to today's governor of Texas from Sam Houston, sharing advice and words of wisdom.

COPY WORK:

Germans settling in the Fredericksburg area worked carefully with neighboring Comanches and signed the successful *Meusebach-Comanche Peace Treaty* with tribal leaders. Read the text of the treaty and pick a section to copy neatly. Decorate your treaty to make it appear official!

http://www.liquisearch.com/meusebach%E2%80%93comanche_treaty/text_of_the_treaty

THE MEXICAN-AMERICAN WAR

pp. 105

VOCABULARY:

ceased, clash, ceded

COMPILING DATA:

Countries who enter war almost always choose to fight for a multitude of reasons, and the Mexican-American War was no exception. Complete the *Two Viewpoints of the Mexican-American War Activity.* List reasons why both the U.S. and Mexico chose to fight this war that eventually changed the map and borders of both Mexico and the U.S. (RB p. 94)

GEOGRAPHY:

Color the land gained after the Mexican-American War on the U.S. map. (RB p. 19)

WRITING:

Create a travel guide which describes and entices travelers to visit the new land gained after the Mexican-American War.

LOOK IT UP:

General Zachary Taylor, American hero of the Mexican-American War, was so admired he soon held another important leadership position. What other important role did he play in U.S. history? (*Answer*: AG p. 104)

WHAT IF?:

What if the Mexican-American War never took place? Do you think the territory acquired by the United States after the war, all the way to the Pacific Ocean, would have remained in Mexico's hands? What would the map/border look like today? How many current states would not be part of the U.S.?

THE TEXAS RANGERS

pp. 106-107

VOCABULARY:

law enforcers, alleviated, revolver, lynch mobs, bandits, raids, bootleggers, jurisdiction, felony, range, intelligence

COPY WORK:

Texas Ranger Napoleon Augustus Jennings participated in the Special Forces search for cattle-rustler and cut-throat John King Fisher and his gang in South Texas. Read his description, pick a paragraph or two to copy, and illustrate:

http://www.eyewitnesstohistory.com/texasrangers.htm

ART:

A. Do some research on the Texas Rangers, then pick one of their many exciting stories to tell on your *Comic Strip* template. (RB p. 37)

B. At www.texasranger.org, you can find some fun stories about fake and replica Texas Ranger badges. Using a thick piece of aluminum foil and a dull pencil, create a new badge for today's Rangers.

WRITING:

Do some research on the Texas Rangers and pick one of the many exciting stories to retell in your own words.

TROUBLE BREWING BETWEEN THE NORTH AND THE SOUTH

pp. 107-109

VOCABULARY:

secessionist, Unionist, ordinance, distraught, impending

CRAFT:

Create the *Slavery Collage.* (RB pp. 98-99)

WRITING:

Sam Houston predicted the secession of the southern states, and with his foresight, said he believed his "beloved South would go down in a sea of blood and smoking ruin." Trace both of your hands on a sheet of paper. On one hand, list five reasons he might have believed Texas should remain with the Union. On the other hand, list five reasons secessionists would have used to try to convince him Texas should secede. Title your page: *Houston's Dilemma*.

COMPARE & CONTRAST:

The decision to secede was not an easy one. Everyone knew the consequences could be dire, and yet some still chose to break away from the U.S. What were they thinking? Put yourself in their shoes, and complete the *Pros and Cons of Secession Activity*. (RB p. 97)

SCIENCE:

Describe the cotton plant and the many uses of its different parts.

COPY WORK:

Have you heard about the *Texas Camel Experiment*? Read and copy one of the daily entries from the primary source report by Lieutenant Echols found on this site:

http://www.texasbob.com/txdoc/texdoc4.html

LOOK IT UP:

The discovery of gold in California resulted in quite a bit of excitement and increased western movement across America. One of the largest nuggets found in California (in 1865) is called the *Fricot Gold Nugget*. Gold (and other precious metals) are weighed and priced by "troy" ounces. The Fricot Nugget weighed 210 troy ounces. How much would the nugget weigh in pounds? (*Answer:* AG p. 104)

CIVIL WAR!

pp. 108-109

VOCABULARY:

enroll, arsenals

CRAFTS:

Add the *Confederate flag* to your *Six Flags Activity Chart*. (RB p. 39)

COOKING:

Try your hand at making *Hard Tack Crackers* (eaten by Union soldiers) and *Johnny Cakes* (eaten by Confederate soldiers). Be careful eating the Hard Track Crackers—they live up to their name! You might want to soak them before eating. Which do you prefer and why? (AG p. 96)

COPY WORK:

Find and copy Abraham Lincoln's *Gettsyburg Address*. Illustrate.

COMPILING DATA:

A. Fill in the **North vs. South Chart.** (RB p. 101; *Answers*: AG p. 112)

B. Use numbers on the face of the clock to learn and remember important facts about the Civil War with the **Civil War Study Clock.** (*Example:* RB p. 95; complete your own RB p. 96)

WHAT IF?:

As you know, Sam Houston was a Southerner (and even a slave owner), but he felt strongly that secession should be avoided at all costs. His name was frequently mentioned as a potential candidate for the President of the United States. *What if* General Houston had been elected President of the United States, prior to the Civil War? He understood both sides of the issue, and some believe he might have been able to avoid the Civil War. What do you think?

THE BATTLE FOR GALVESTON

p. 109

VOCABULARY:

bypassing, cotton bales, blockade runners

WRITING:

The Civil War was filled with tragic stories of families who had members fighting on opposite sides of the war. Read the story of Lt. Commander Edward Lea and Albert Lea and the *Battle for Galveston*, easily found online. Write a poem or song lyrics about this touching, sad tale of war.

LOOK IT UP:

Did the warships *Bayou City* and *Neptune* belong to the Union or Confederate Navy? (AG p. 104)

THE BATTLE OF SABINE PASS

pp. 109-110

VOCABULARY:

campaign (military), *gunboats*

BATTLE NEAR BROWNSVILLE

p. 110

VOCABULARY:

teamsters, disruption

WRITING:

Write a public service announcement to be given by the mayor at the site of the battle.

KEEPING UNION FORCES AT BAY

p. 110

ART:

Tell the story of Civil War battles in Texas using your **Comic Strip** template. (RB p. 37)

LIFE IN TEXAS DURING THE CIVIL WAR

pp. 110-112

VOCABULARY:

homespun

GEOGRAPHY:

Label the sites of *Civil War Battles* on a U.S. map. (RB p. 100; map RB p. 19)

COPY WORK:

Texas was fortunate few battles took place within the state. Other states were not so lucky. A ten-year-old girl named Carrie Berry lived in Atlanta, Georgia, during the Civil War. Pick a day, copy her entry, and illustrate:

https://www.nps.gov/saga/learn/education/upload/Carrie%20Berry%20Diary.pdf

THE CIVIL WAR IS OVER

p. 112

VOCABULARY:

enforced, advantage

LOOK IT UP:

How much time had passed between the *Emancipation Proclamation* and *Juneteenth* (1865)? (*Answer*: AG p. 104)

MATH:

Make a graph comparing the total casualties from the following wars which involved either Texas or the United States; include the Civil War, World War I, World War II, Korea, Vietnam, and the Gulf War.

WHAT IF:

What if the South had won the war?

COPY WORK:

Copy General Granger's proclamation that slaves were now free, given on the first "Juneteenth" in 1865 in Galveston. (AG p. 99)

RECONSTRUCTION

pp. 112-113

VOCABULARY:

Reconstruction, assassination, outlaw, proclamation, Juneteenth

LOOK IT UP:

According to the Thirteenth Amendment, slavery and involuntary servitude shall not exist in the United States, except under what circumstances? (*Answer*: AG p. 104)

WRITING:

Following the Civil War, Americans faced a great deal of change, whether they were landowners or freed slaves. Write a *quatrain*-style poem about change. (Instructions are easily found online.)

COMPILING DATA:

The Civil War changed the lives of all Americans. How did the war affect African American slaves? Complete the *For Better or Worse Activity* (RB pp. 102-03)

NEW RULES FOR STATEHOOD

pp. 113-114

VOCABULARY:

impeach, misconduct, convict

COPY WORK:

John H. Reagan served as Postmaster General for the Confederacy and was imprisoned in Boston for a time after the Civil War ended. From his cell, Reagan sent an open letter to the people of Texas, advising the state to cooperate with the federal government. Copy this portion of the letter as you imagine sitting in a dark cell, perhaps the only light coming from a candle or a small window. (AG p. 100)

WRITING:

New rules were enacted after the Civil War to ensure peace and stability. Sit down with your family and create a list of house rules. Does everyone in your family agree to ratify these rules?

WHAT IF?

What would have happened if the South had refused to follow the Union's guidelines to ensure future statehood? How would the Union have solved this problem?

TEXAS AFTER RECONSTRUCTION

p. 114

LOOK IT UP:

Certain Texans labeled some of Governor Davis's legislative programs the "Obnoxious Acts." What were these acts and why were some concerned about these programs? Can you think of any current government programs, people, or laws you would label obnoxious? Why? (AG p. 104)

SCIENCE:

What three inventions impacted the cotton industry the most? Who were the inventors and how did their inventions change farming?

WRITING:

Read the Thirteenth, Fourteenth, and Fifteenth Amendments to the Constitution and then the Emancipation Proclamation. What words stand out? How does word choice impact the overall tone of a document?

UNIT TEST:

Complete the *Statehood and Civil War Unit Test.* (RB pp. 130-31; *Answers*: p. 102)

WRITING
PROMPT
PAGE 127

SUGGESTED READING:

Let's Remember Texas, the 28th State by Betsy Warren

The Lone Star State Divided by Merle Durham

Civil War in Texas and New Mexico Territory by Steve Cottrell

Texas Rangers: Legendary Lawmen by Michael P. Spradlin

Lone Star Legacy: The Texas Rangers Then and Now by Melanie Chrismer

A Paradise Called Texas (and sequels) by Janice Shefelman

John Barclay Armstrong: Texas Ranger by Judy Alter

Little Women by Louisa May Alcott

The Mexican-American War by Ruth Tenzer Feldman

ART TO EXPLORE:

The Annexation of Texas by Donald M. Yena
The Republic of Texas is No More - lithograph
Texas Coming In – political cartoon by H. Bucholzer
James P. Henderson by William H. Huddle
American Progress (Manifest Destiny) by John Gast
Hood's Texas Brigade by Don Troiani
Lasting Friendship Statue in Fredericksburg sculpted by J. Hester

WEBSITES:

Civil War in Texas: http://www.civilwartraveler.com/TRANS/TX/
Civil War in Texas: https://www.nps.gov//abpp/battles/txmap.htm
Texas Rangers: https://www.dps.texas.gov/texasrangers/
Texas Rangers: http://www.texasranger.org/index.htm
Mexican-American War: www.pbs.org/kera/usmexicanwar/index_flash.html
Mexican-American War: http://library.uta.edu/usmexicowar/
African Americans in Texas:
https://texastimetravel.oncell.com/en/african-americans-in-texas-57132.html

VIDEOS:

Texas in the Civil War

http://www.thc.texas.gov/historic-sites/sabine-pass-battleground/history/video

MUSIC AND SONGS:

Spirituals were beautiful songs written and sung by slaves as they worked and yearned for freedom. Look for a few of these songs online and note how many are still sung today: "Go Down, Moses," "Let Us Break Bread Together," "Swing Low, Sweet Chariot," and "There is a Balm in Gilead."

✶✶✶✶✶✶

Other Civil War era songs include:
"When Johnny Comes Marching Home" by Patrick Gilmore
"The Battle Hymn of the Republic" by Julia Ward Howe
"I Wish I Was in Dixie" by Daniel Decatur Emmett
"Camptown Races," "Oh! Susanna!," and "Jeanie With the Light Brown Hair" by Stephen Foster

IT'S ABOUT TIME! Game suggestions:

Polk signs resolution and Texas becomes 28th state in the Union (December, 1845), Mexican-American War begins (May, 1846), Treaty of Guadalupe Hidalgo (February, 1848), California admitted to the Union as a free state (1850), Texas secedes from Union (1861), Union Navy captures Galveston (1862), Battle of Sabine Pass (September, 1863), Civil War ends (May, 1865), Texas readmitted to the Union (1870)

Twenty Questions and Memory Game Suggestions:

President James K Polk, J. Pinckney Henderson, General Zachary Taylor, Big Foot Wallace, Jack Hayes, Abraham Lincoln, Jefferson Davis, General John B. Magruder, Colonel Rip Ford, Ulysses S. Grant, James W. Throckmorton, Richard Coke, the Texas Rangers, "Three-legged Willie" Williamson, Robert E. Lee, President Andrew Johnson, General Gordon Granger

PLACES TO VISIT:

Sabine Pass Battleground State Historic Site - Port Arthur, Texas
Texas Civil War Museum – Fort Worth
Fort Davis National Historic Site – Fort Davis
Camp Ford – Tyler
Texas Ranger Hall of Fame and Museum – Waco
Texas State Capitol – Austin
Historic Fort Stockton – Fort Stockton
Palo Alto Battlefield National Historic Site – Brownsville
Pioneer Museum – Fredericksburg
Vereins Kirche Museum - Fredericksburg

SUPPLY LIST:
- ingredients for *Peanut Brittle, Hard Tack, and Johnny Cake* recipes
- thick aluminum foil

TEXAS NATIVE AMERICANS AFTER THE CIVIL WAR

pp. 115-116

VOCABULARY:

> *buffalo hunters, muzzle-loading pistols, access, comply*

VOCABULARY WINDOWPANE:

> Complete the *Vocabulary Windowpane* using the vocabulary words above, and continue to add vocabulary words throughout the unit. (RB p. 33)

KWL:

> Begin the *KWL Chart* on Texas Cowboys and Indians. Once you have completed the unit, don't forget to add notes about what you learned in the final "L" column. (RB p. 35)

COMPILING DATA:

> Fill in the *A to Z Chart* about Cowboys and Indians as you proceed through this unit. (RB p. 21)

MATH:

> *Timeline*: Fill in important dates on the timeline as you proceed through this unit. (RB p. 41)

COPY WORK:

> In 1889, Dagmar Mariager participated in a buffalo hunt. Copy the beautiful language he uses to describe his first encounter with the buffalo, up close. (AG p. 100)

THE PLAINS INDIANS ATTACK

pp. 116

VOCABULARY:

> *mediator*

LOOK IT UP:

> Who is described as the "Last Chief of the Comanche?" (*Answer*: AG p. 104)

NATIVE AMERICANS ON THE RIO GRANDE

p. 117

VOCABULARY:

> *buffalo soldiers*

LOOK IT UP:

> What other duties did Buffalo Soldiers have besides their military work? (*Answer*: AG p. 104)

COPY WORK:

> A. Read more about the Buffalo Soldiers in "The Buffalo Soldier" by Larry Francell (in *The Portal to Texas History*) and select a paragraph to copy and illustrate on the daily life of the soldiers.
> **https://texashistory.unt.edu/ark:/67531/metapth45386/m1/42/sizes/?q=%22buffalo%2soldiers%22**

B. Search for Remington's account, "A Scout With the Buffalo Soldiers," and pick a paragraph to copy and illustrate. (First published in *The Century*, Volume 37, Issue 6, 1889: 902.)

CATTLE BUSINESS AND RANCHING

pp. 117-119

VOCABULARY:

corralled, Texas longhorns, open range, vaqueros, branding, mustangs, lasso, barbed wire fence, rangeland, windmills, surplus, decline

CRAFT:

Have you ever made a potato print? Use this method to make your own "cattle brand." Cut a potato in half, and after designing your personal "brand," use a sharp pencil to lightly draw the 3-D design in the center of the cut side of the potato. Carve out the excess potato around the edges of your design, leaving a raised, three dimensional "brand." Dip your brand in paint and stamp away! You can make cards, wrapping paper . . . you name it!

WRITING:

Tall Tales have been a part of American folklore for generations. You've probably read stories about Paul Bunyon, but have you heard of Pecos Bill? Find books or stories online about this amazing (and wildly exaggerated) Texas cowboy, then write your own tall tale. Next time you sit around the family campfire or firepit, share the tale with your audience. Be dramatic!

MATH:

An average cow weighs between 1,000 and 1,800 pounds. Most cows will eat at least two pounds of hay daily for each 100 lbs of their body weight. Calculate the amount of hay needed per day for a 1,000 lb, 1,200 lb, and 1,700 lb cow. (*Answer:* AG p. 108)

GEOGRAPHY:

Complete the *Cattle Trail Map Activity* (RB p. 106), using the U.S. map (RB p. 19).

COWBOY LIFE

pp. 118-119

VOCABULARY:

stockyards, drovers, wrangler, rustlers, isolate, cowhands

WRITING:

A *limerick* is a 5-line poem with a specific rhythm and rhyme scheme. Research the proper way to write a limerick, then create your own about the life of a cowboy.

CRAFT:

A. In the old days, cowboy boots were designed to serve as work shoes with a purpose. Today, they are often just a fashion statement and can be very expensive. Design your own pair of cowboy boots reflecting your personality. (RB p. 105)

B. Use a *Comic Strip* template to reveal the life of a cowboy. (RB p. 37)

SCIENCE:

Beef is the primary product derived from cattle, but there are many other by-products (something else that comes from making the main product) produced for consumption. Make a list of these products and categorize them on a *T-Chart* as edible and non-edible beef products. (RB p. 27)

COPY WORK:

Pick one of the cowboy songs from the "Music and Songs" on page 74, find the song online, and copy the lyrics. Illustrate!

FARMING

p. 120

VOCABULARY:

dry farming, plantation, tenant farmer, sharecropper

LOOK IT UP:

What is a commodity? Look up ten of Texas's most important commodities today. (*Answer*: AG p. 104)   **http://www.texasagriculture.gov/About/TexasAgStats.aspx**

CHANGE AND PROGRESS CLOSE OUT THE 19TH CENTURY

pp. 120-22

VOCABULARY:

hired hands, allotted, stances, conservative, segregated, dedicated, commerce, pavement, gristmills, textile, meat packing, cottonseed oil, mining, surged, monopoly, free trade, antitrust laws, streetcars

LOOK IT UP:

Name two uses for the cotton by-product, cottonseed oil. (*Answer*: AG p. 104)

WRITING:

Complete the *Identify Fact versus Opinion Activity.* (RB p. 104)

UNIT TEST:

Complete the *Cowboys and Indians Unit Test.* (RB pp. 132-33; *Answers*: AG p. 102)

SUGGESTED READING:

THC Pamphlet: The Chisolm Trail: http://www.thc.texas.gov/explore-texas
The Chisolm Trail in American History by William R. Sanford
Trail Fever: The Life of a Texas Cowboy by D.J. Lightfoot
Pecos Bill by Steven Kellogg
The Texas Cowboy's Journal: Up the Trail to Kansas in 1868 by Jack Bailey (this is an actual journal written by a real cowboy in 1868)
The Coldest Day in Texas by Peggy Purser Freeman (historical fiction)
Buckaroo Poetry: Cowboy Poems for Young and Old by P.W. Conway

ART TO EXPLORE:

The Great Royal Buffalo Hunt by Louis Maurer
Albumen Portrait Photo of Quanah Parker (unknown photographer)
Mackenzie's Raiders at Palo Duro by Michael Gray
The Bronco Buster by Frederic Remington
Cattle Drive by Charles M. Russell

WEBSITES:

King Ranch History: https://king-ranch.com/about-us/history/
Buffalo Soldiers: www.buffalosoldier.net
Texas Independence Trail/Cowboy Culture: http://texasindependencetrail.com/node/23785
The Chisolm Trail:
https://texastimetravel.oncell.com/en/the-chisholm-trail-exploring-the-folklore-and-legacy-134179.html
The Red River War: https://texastimetravel.oncell.com/en/red-river-war-of-1874-1875-72624.html

MUSIC AND SONGS:

Cowboy Music and Poetry (You can find examples of Red Steagall's poetry online.)
"Back in the Saddle Again" by Gene Autry and Ray Whitley
"Home on the Range" by Brewster Higley
"Git Along Little Dogies" – traditional cowboy ballad
"Tumbling Tumbleweeds" by Bob Nolan
"Cattle Call" by Tex Owens
"Happy Trails" by Dale Evans
"Don't Fence Me In" by Cole Porter
Most of these songs are twentieth century references to cowboy life.

MOVIES AND DOCUMENTARIES:

Tall Tale: The Unbelievable Adventures of Pecos Bill (1995)

WRITING
PROMPT
PAGE 129

Twenty Questions and Memory Game Suggestions:

*Quanah Parker, Colonel Ranald Mackenzie, Chief Victorio,
Colonel Benjamin H. Grierson, Richard King, Charles Goodnight,
General William Tecumseh Sherman, Chief Satanta, Oran M. Roberts, Elisabet Ney,
drover, wrangler, sharecropper*

IT'S ABOUT TIME! Game suggestions:

Battle of Adobe Walls (June 1874), Battle of Palo Duro Canyon (September 1874), the Texas capitol burns (1881), new capitol dedicated (1888), Texas Railroad Commission established (1891), Texas Constitution that is still in effect today was written (1876), long distance telephone service available in Texas (1883), anti-trust law passed to protect smaller businesses (1889)

PLACES TO VISIT:

King Ranch – Kingsville
Buffalo Soldiers National Museum – Houston
National Ranching Heritage Center – Lubbock
George Ranch Historical Park – Richmond
Frontier Texas! – Abilene
Museum of Western Art – Kerrville
Sid Richardson Museum – Fort Worth
The Stockyards Museum – Fort Worth
Red Steagall's Annual Cowboy Gathering and Western Swing Festival - Fort Worth
National Cowgirl Museum and Hall of Fame - Fort Worth
Dude Ranches – Bandera, Graham, and other locations
Tejas Rodeo Company – Bulverde
XIT Museum - Dalhart
Texas State Railroad Historical Park - Rusk

SUPPLY LIST:

- potato
- knife
- paint

THE NEW CENTURY OPENS: TEXAS IN THE 1900s

p. 123

VOCABULARY:

seawall, thriving

VOCABULARY WINDOWPANE:

Complete the *Vocabulary Windowpane* using the vocabulary words above, and continue to add vocabulary words throughout the unit. (RB p. 33)

KWL:

Begin the *KWL Chart* regarding Texas in the 20th Century. Once you have completed the unit, don't forget to add notes about what you learned in the final "L" column. (RB p. 35)

COMPILING DATA:

Fill in the *A to Z Chart* about Texas in the 1900s as you proceed through this unit. (RB p. 21)

MATH:

Timeline: Fill in important dates on the timeline as you proceed through this unit. (RB p. 41)

COPY WORK:

Find the firsthand account of the **Great Galveston Storm of 1900** written by Isaac Cline, the city's chief meteorologist. He describes the weather leading up to the storm, the storm itself, and the aftermath. Copy a paragraph and illustrate the scene. Here's one source of his account:

http://www.eyewitnesstohistory.com/galveston.htm

WRITING:

Write a dramatic story about a person your age experiencing the Great Storm of 1900 in Galveston. Illustrate.

SCIENCE:

In order to help protect their island in future hurricanes, Galvestonians built a seawall and raised the level of the island 17 feet. How did they accomplish this feat? Where did the fill sand come from, and how were they able to fill it in under existing houses? You'll find some old photographs of this huge achievement here:

http://www.gthcenter.org/exhibits/graderaising/index.html

WHAT IF?:

What if Galvestonians had *not* chosen to stay and rebuild after the Great Storm of 1900? What would have happened to Galveston? What would the island look like today?

OIL!

p. 124

VOCABULARY:

tar, kerosene, petroleum, refinery, crude oil, quadrupled, ocean tankers, boomtown, support industries, lucrative, oil derrick, efficient, retail, manufacture, lubricant

SCIENCE:

Energy sources are either renewable or non-renewable. List five sources of renewable and five sources of non-renewable energy. Then do a little research and note several advantages and disadvantages of both.

CRAFT/WRITING:

There are several websites dedicated to creating word clouds. Write a short paragraph about oil, its source, and its uses. Plug your writing in the word cloud. Voila!

COPY WORK:

Find a list of the first twenty major oil discoveries in Texas, beginning with the oil field in Corsicana (1894). Copy the name of each oil field and the date neatly on a chart. Here is one source:

http://texasalmanac.com/topics/business/oil-and-texas-cultural-history

COMPILING DATA:

Fill in the giant oil drops about the Texas oil industry on the *Oil in Texas* activity. There is only enough space to write the most important information, so be efficient! (RB p. 111)

WHERE DO OIL AND NATURAL GAS COME FROM?

pp. 124-25

VOCABULARY:

microscopic, organisms, carbon molecules, drilling rigs, reservoirs, diesel fuel, non-renewable energy, renewable energy, solar energy, fossil fuels

LOOK IT UP:

Fossil fuels include crude oil, natural gas, and coal. These three are considered non-renewable energy sources. Another non-renewable fuel is uranium ore. Is uranium ore a fossil fuel? What type of power plants use uranium ore as fuel? (*Answer*: AG p. 104)

SCIENCE:

Create a tri-fold chart (fold a paper into equal thirds) about fossil fuels, labeling each section: crude oil, natural gas, and coal. In each section, show the source of each fuel, how they are obtained from the ground, and how they are used to provide energy.

ART:

Create a *Comic Strip* explaining how ancient organisms become products of oil we use today. (RB p. 37)

CHANGES FOR WOMEN AND MINORITIES

pp. 125-26

VOCABULARY:

women's suffrage, primaries, general election, segregated, poll tax, enrollment, chaos, discrimination, pendulum

POETRY:

Inside the lady's hat, write a *shape poem* about women in the first two decades of the 20th century or about the women's suffrage movement. (RB p. 107) For fun examples of other shape poems, please see:

www.youngwriters.co.uk/types-shape-poem
www.shadowpoetry.com/resources/wip/shape.html

WRITING:

People often expressed their support of women's suffrage through music and plays. Erminia Thompson Folsom wrote such lyrics, to be sung to the tune of "Dixie," in 1917. You can find these lyrics online (the song is entitled "Woman's Rights in Texas"). See if you can match the words to the music. Then write your own lyrics to a new song about either women's right to vote or another inequality you have noticed and would like to see changed.

WHAT IF?:

What if women had always been allowed to vote? Do you think their additional votes would have made a difference in the officials elected? Would different presidents have meant a different history for our state and country? How? Do you believe men and women vote differently? Why or why not?

WORLD WAR ONE

pp. 126-27

VOCABULARY:

imperialism, alliances, heir, neutral, diplomat, war bonds, rationing, code talking, general armistice

COPY WORK:

Find a copy of the beautiful poem, "In Flanders Fields" by John McCrae. To illustrate, search for one of artist Georgia O'Keeffe's (she lived in Texas for a time) paintings of a poppy and do your best to copy her style.

GENEALOGY:

Most families have stories about parents, grandparents, aunts, or uncles who have participated in some war in the history of our nation. Talk to your parents and make a list of your relatives who have served or are currently serving in the military. Then make a "Veteran Family Tree," including their names, branch of service, and time period of their service, to honor these brave men and women.

GEOGRAPHY:

Using a world map, find the following countries: (Allies: Great Britain, France, Russia, Italy, the United States) and the Central Powers (Germany, Bulgaria, Austria-Hungary, Ottoman Empire). Since boundaries and countries have changed since World War I, search online for a map specific to the World War I time period.

CRAFT:

During the war, Americans volunteered to help with the scarcity of food overseas by rationing particular foods at home. Research "food rationing in World War I" online and find five types of food Americans used sparingly, so the excess could be sent to our soldiers and allies.
Then find some historic food rationing posters online, pretend you lived during World War I, and create your own slogan and sign to encourage rationing with your fellow citizens.

TEXAS FOLLOWING WORLD WAR ONE

p. 128

VOCABULARY:

prosper, drastically, panicked, supply versus demand, broadcasting

LOOK IT UP:

Find the name of the German diplomat who wrote the Zimmerman Telegram. (*Answer*: AG p. 104)

WHAT IF?:

What if the United States had never entered World War I and assisted their European allies? Would the war have ended differently? What would Europe look like now?

THE GREAT DEPRESSION

pp. 128-29

VOCABULARY:

stock market, shares, invested, shareholders, profit, wildcatters, droves, stable, overproduction, surpluses

MATH:

Research the cost of living during the Great Depression (1930s). How much was the value of one dollar at that time compared to the value of one dollar today? With that knowledge, create a chart with the cost of the following items during the 1930s versus the cost of these items today: *a loaf of bread, a car, a middle-class home, a bicycle, a pound of hamburger, a soda, a light bulb, a pair of jeans, a gallon of gas, a dozen eggs, and a baseball.*

WHAT IF?:

What if you had been alive during the Great Depression? What would you and your family have done to protect your home and your family from hunger?

THE DUST BOWL

p. 129

VOCABULARY:

plow, erosion, migrated

WRITING:

Find the wonderful 20-minute video, "Jack and the Dust Bowl," online. After watching the movie, write your own story about an innovation that comes about during a difficult time.

SCIENCE:

Many lessons were learned about farming and erosion after America's experience with the Dust Bowl. Research and write a short paper on the practices that led to this disaster, the lessons learned, and the changes which were put in place following this difficult period in our nation's history.

COPY WORK:

Ann Marie Lowe lived in North Dakota during the dust bowl days and kept a diary during that time. You can easily find her diary entries online. Pick a daily entry, copy in your best writing, and illustrate.

THE NEW DEAL

pp. 129-30

VOCABULARY:

conserve, structures, compensated, windbreaks, alternating crops, Centennial

LOOK IT UP:

List ten projects or programs created by the New Deal to help Americans during the Great Depression.

ART:

A. Between 1935-1943, one of the New Deal programs was created to help artists who produced 15,663 paintings, murals, sculptures, and more for public buildings around the country. Many of these can still be seen in small towns in Texas today. Design a mural which could be painted on a wall in your town today.

TEXAS AND WORLD WAR TWO

pp. 130-31

VOCABULARY:

economic, prisoner of war camps, vital, magnesium, synthetic rubber, victory gardens, appliances, communism, regime

WRITING:

An *ode* is a short poem written in praise of a person or thing. Find some examples of odes and enjoy the beautiful imagery. Then write your own "Ode to a Soldier" in honor of a family member or perhaps even an unknown veteran who served and sacrificed in time of war.

COPY WORK:

World War II soldiers often mailed and received letters to and from their family waiting at home. In fact, this particular soldier even decorated the envelope with colorful drawings of the landscape and animals he discovered where he was stationed. Copy this short excerpt from one of his letters, and then decorate the outside of an envelope as he might have done. (AG p. 100)

WHAT IF?:

We'll ask you the same question we asked after you read about World War I: *What if* the United States had never entered World War II and assisted their European allies? Would the war have ended differently? What would Europe and Asia look like now? Which countries would be friends, and which would be enemies?

TEXAS AFTER WORLD WAR TWO

pp. 131-32

VOCABULARY:

decisive, capitalist, demilitarized

WRITING:

Interview someone who was alive during the Civil Rights movement in the 1960s. Ask them about the many changes they observed over time. Take notes, then write a short essay about these changes.

LOOK IT UP:

What was the Highway Beautification Act? (*Answer*: AG p. 104)

ART:

A. Show how Texas and Texans assisted our country in the war efforts using a *Comic Strip* template. (RB p. 37)

B. President Johnson's wife, Claudia Alta ("Lady Bird"), was instrumental in beautifying our state with her plan to seed the areas near highways with wildflowers, particularly bluebonnets. In the spring, Texas residents can be found all over, taking photos of the beautiful scenery. Use a camera and take some photos of wildflowers native to your area. Print and put them together in a pleasing collage.

CITIES AND HIGHWAYS

pp. 132-33

VOCABULARY:

interstate, suburbs, vacuum tubes, transistor, portable, chips, integrated silicon circuit, promoter, artificial satellite, fertilizer, insecticide, mechanization, feedlots, meat processing

Math:

Fold a paper into three equal sections. In the first column, create a timeline with the approximate dates of the invention of the following modes of transportation: *walking, canoe, sailboat, steamboat, motorboat, railroad train, airplane, automobile, subway train, bicycle, supersonic jet, space shuttle.* In the next column, note the typical speed (in miles per hour) of the vehicle.

In a third column, note how many miles the vehicle could travel in 12 hours.

Craft:

Design a new mode of transportation to be developed in 20 years. What fuel does it use? How is it made? What would you name it? Design your vehicle on paper, and then make a small-scale, three-dimensional version with legos or other materials.

Science:

Using a *T-Chart* (RB p. 27), list the following forms of transportation in the left column, and the type of energy and fuel used to make the vehicle move in the right column: *bicycle, train (there will be several fuel sources for trains), automobile, canoe, steamboat, cruise ship, airplane, tractor, bus, skateboard, subway train, tram, helicopter, rickshaw, trolley, glider, elevator, escalator, motorboat, gondola, dirigible, boogie board, horse, dogsled, sailboat, bobsled, covered wagon, and jet ski.*

Writing:

Research typical words, slang, and phrases from the 1940s that we don't often hear today. Write a story set during that time period, using your newly-discovered lingo in the tale.

TEXAS AND THE COLD WAR

pp. 133-34

Vocabulary:

defectors, missiles, nuclear weapon plants, geologists, petroleum engineers

Writing:

Write a biography detailing the life and accomplishments of an interesting Texan who has made a difference in the state and the world.

Science:

Texans Dr. Michael DeBakey and Dr. Denton Cooley were pioneers in the field of creating and implanting a completely artificial heart. Why might someone need an artificial heart? Draw a diagram of a human heart and then a diagram of an artificial heart. What is the longest number of years a patient has lived with an artificial heart?

Game:

Play *"I Have, Who Has" Twentieth Century Game.* (RB pp. 108-10; *Answers*: AG p. 108-9) See instructions for game directions on p. 52 of this book, using Anthony Lucas as the opening card.

Look It Up:

What is the price of crude oil today? Has the recent price gone up or down? (*Answer*: AG p. 104)

Unit Test:

Complete the *Texas in the Twentieth Century Unit Test* (RB pp. 134-35; *Answers*: AG p. 102)

ART TO EXPLORE:

Oveta Culp Hobby by Seymour Stone
Spindletop Viewing Her Gusher by Aaron Arion
Miriam A. Ferguson by Lucy Rice
Drouth Stricken Area by Alexander Hogue
Dust Bowl by Alexander Hogue

SUGGESTED READING:

Oveta Culp Hobby by Debra L. Winegarten
Isaac's Storm by Erik Larson (teens/adults)
Galveston's Summer of the Storm by Julie Lake (historical fiction)
The Grapes of Wrath by John Steinbeck (historical fiction) [teens/adults]
Thimble Summer by Elizabeth Enright

WEBSITES:

Oil and Gas:
http://www.adventuresinenergy.org/What-are-Oil-and-Natural-Gas/How-Are-Oil-Natural-Gas-Formed.html
Oil and Gas: http://texasalmanac.com/topics/business/oil-and-texas-cultural-history
Oil and Gas: www.oceanstaroec.com *and*
www.thestoryoftexas.com/discover/campfire-stories/roughneck
World War I:
http://www.thc.texas.gov/preserve/projects-and-programs/state-historical-markers/thematic-marker-maps/texas-world-war-i
Texas Archive of the Moving Image: http://texasarchive.org/starringthelonestarstate/
Battleship Texas: http://tpwd.texas.gov/state-parks/battleship-texas/park_history
World War I: https://www.theworldwar.org/education
Women's Right to Vote: https://www.tsl.texas.gov/lobbyexhibits/struggles-women
Civilian Conservation Corps Coloring Book: https://teachingtexas.org/resources/coloring-ccc

MOVIES AND DOCUMENTARIES:

Jack and the Dustbowl (2012) Whitestone Motion Pictures
World War I:
https://texastimetravel.oncell.com/en/world-war-i-texas-and-the-great-war-136851.html
World War II:
https://texastimetravel.oncell.com/en/world-war-ii-on-the-texas-home-front-91541.html

Twenty Questions and Memory Game Suggestions:

Anthony Lucas, William P. Hobby, Archduke Ferdinand, President Herbert Hoover, President Franklin D. Roosevelt, Miriam Ferguson, Adolf Hitler, Emperor Hirohito, General Dwight Eisenhower, Oveta Culp Hobby, Lyndon Baines Johnson, President John F. Kennedy, Lady Bird Johnson, President George W. Bush, President George H.W. Bush, President Dwight D. Eisenhower, Justice Sandra Day O'Connor, Congresswoman Barbara Jordan, President Woodrow Wilson, seawall, Spindletop, NASA

IT'S ABOUT TIME! Game suggestions:

The Great Galveston Storm/Hurricane (September, 1900), Spindletop gusher (January, 1901), Women received right to vote with the 19th amendment (1920), World War I begins (1914), Treaty of Versailles officially ends World War I (1919), Stock Market Crash (1920), Centennial Celebrations of Texas Independence (1936), Pearl Harbor bombed and U.S. enters World War II (1941), World War II ends (1945), Korean War begins (1950), Vietnam War begins (1955), Interstate Highway System begins (1956), Gulf War begins (1990)

PLACES TO VISIT:

Spindletop Gladys City Boomtown Museum – Beaumont
East Texas Oil Museum – Kilgore
Central Texas Oil Patch Museum - Luling
Pier 21 Theater and Movie "The Great Storm" – Galveston
The Ocean Star Offshore Drilling Rig/Museum - Galveston
Seawall – Galveston
Galveston Railroad Museum - Galveston
Battleship Texas State Historic Site – La Porte
Call Field Aviation Museum – Wichita Falls
Fort Sam Houston Museum – Fort Sam Houston (San Antonio)
Museum of the American G.I. – College Station
Texas Military Forces Museum at Camp Mabry – Austin
National Museum of the Pacific War – Fredericksburg
Frontiers of Flight Museum – Dallas
Old Jail and Gallows – Gonzales
The Sixth-Floor Museum – Dallas
Space Center Houston - Clear Lake
Lyndon B. Johnson State Park and Historic Park – Stonewall
Sauer-Beckmann Farm - Stonewall
Dr. Pepper Museum – Waco
George Bush Presidential Library and Museum – College Station
George W. Bush Presidential Library and Museum - Dallas
Sam Houston Ship Channel Boat Tour - Houston

WRITING PROMPT PAGE 131

SUPPLY LIST:
- red paint
- world map depicting countries as they were during World War I and II
- camera

UNIT 11: TEXAS GOVERNMENT TODAY
Activities and Resources

WHO WE ARE AND WHERE WE LIVE

pp. 135-37

VOCABULARY:

public official, crawfish, pow wow, stock show, reenactments, incorporated, shindigs

VOCABULARY WINDOWPANE:

Complete the *Vocabulary Windowpane* using the vocabulary words above, and continue to add vocabulary words throughout the unit. (RB p. 33)

KWL:

Begin the *KWL Chart* on Texas Government Today. Once you have completed the unit, don't forget to add notes about what you learned in the final "L" column. (RB p. 35)

COMPILING DATA:

Fill in the *A to Z Chart* about Texas Government Today as you proceed through this unit. (RB p. 21)

LOOK IT UP:

Find the populations for Texas's largest and smallest cities. (*Answer*: AG p. 105)

One source: **https://www.tsl.texas.gov/ref/abouttx/popcity6.html**

COMPILING DATA:

Create a chart of Texas professional sports teams. Include football, basketball, baseball, soccer, and hockey. Don't forget to research the names of women's teams as well!

ART:

Research ten popular festivals held in Texas each year. Create a travel brochure inviting guests to attend these celebrations. Be sure to include a map and note the cities where the festivals are held.

TEXAS GOVERNMENT TODAY

p. 137

VOCABULARY:

federalism, regulate commerce, function, limits, amending

COPY WORK:

Copy the Tenth Amendment to the United States Constitution. Discuss what this means for the powers of each of the fifty states. **www.archives.gov/founding-docs/bill-of-rights-transcript**

THE TEXAS CONSTITUTION

p. 137

VOCABULARY:

checks and balances, override, unconstitutional

COPY WORK:

Find and read the Bill of Rights in the Texas Constitution. Copy what you believe is one of the most important amendments. Do you see any similarities between the Texas and the United States Constitution's Bill of Rights? You can find the Texas Bill of Rights here:

http://www.statutes.legis.state.tx.us/SOTWDocs/CN/htm/CN.1.htm

THE THREE BRANCHES OF GOVERNMENT

Legislative

pp. 138-40

VOCABULARY:

budget, inhabitants, interpret, bicameral, appropriate (verb), drafting, proposals, resolution, bill, debates

LOOK IT UP:

Who represents your district in the Texas House of Representatives and Texas Senate? Be sure to keep a record of their names, phone numbers, and emails for your records. You can begin by filling out the *My Representatives* chart. (RB p. 114)

Executive

VOCABULARY:

appointed, eligible, appointees

LOOK IT UP:

Find the names of the current the Texas governor, lieutenant governor, and attorney general. Write down their names, phone numbers, and email for future reference. (RB p. 114)

WRITING:

Research and write a one-page biography covering the life of Texas's current governor.

Judicial

VOCABULARY:

criminal, civil, enforced, procedures, juries, civil law, criminal code, felony, misdemeanor, jury duty, grand jury, indictment, petit jury, plea bargain, appeals court, verdicts, rendered

LOOK IT UP:

List the nine current justices of the Texas Supreme Court and the years in which they began serving. Note which justice serves as the Chief Justice of the court.

COMPILING DATA:

Complete the *Three Branches of the Government Activity*. (RB pp. 112-13)

TEXAS REPRESENTATIVES IN WASHINGTON, D.C.

p. 140

VOCABULARY:

republic, federal, constituents

LOOK IT UP:

Find the two Texas senators and your congressman/woman who serves in the United States House of Representatives in Washington, D.C. Be sure to record their contact information. (RB p. 114)

THE STATE CAPITAL AND CAPITOL

pp. 140-43

VOCABULARY:

capital, capitol, Capitol, rotunda, mosaic

LOOK IT UP:

Research and list ten statues found on the Texas capitol grounds. Which is your favorite?

ART:

Choose one of the statues listed above to illustrate or recreate with clay.

LOCAL GOVERNMENT

pp. 144-46

VOCABULARY:

rural, local community

LOOK IT UP:

How is your city government set up? Who are the leaders and those who represent you? Record these names and contact information.

City Government

VOCABULARY:

general law, home rule, personnel, maintenance, tax assessor, appraises, remits

County Government

VOCABULARY:

county courthouse, records, commissioners court, precincts, bonds

LOOK IT UP:

Find your county courthouse. What year was it built? What offices are located within the courthouse?

COMPILING DATA:

Find and circle your county on the *Texas Counties Map* (RB p. 17). Next, find your completed Region Map from Unit Two. Using the *Region Map* as a guide, do your best to draw the region borders on the *Counties Map*. Color each region a different color lightly over the county names that fall within each region.

Special Districts

VOCABULARY:

rapid transit, school district, school board

LOOK IT UP:

Look up the names of your local Special Districts. What purposes do they serve?

COMPILING DATA:

Complete the *Levels of Government* activity. (RB p. 112; *Answers*: AG p. 109)

YOU CAN MAKE A DIFFERENCE!

p. 146

VOCABULARY:

moral, endeavored, condemned, forefathers, native-born, naturalized, resident, general election, vacancies, bond proposal, ballot, align

ART:

Pretend that you are running for a local or state political office. Which office would that be? Design a brochure to convince fellow Texans you are the man or woman for the job! Be sure and tell your fellow citizens what you plan to do to make Texas an even better state.

YOUR NECK OF THE WOODS

p. 147

LOOK IT UP:

In your Reproducible Book, on p. 115 you will find an *Information Scavenger Hunt* for your own city or town. Fill in the blanks by researching the answers online or with personal interviews.

ART:

Either find a picture of your county courthouse online, or take a trip and visit the actual courthouse. Sketch a picture of the courthouse and grounds. Be sure to include any statues which might be nearby of local or state heroes.

UNIT TEST:

Complete the *Texas Government Today Unit Test* (RB pp. 136-37; *Answers*: AG p. 102)

FINAL ACTIVITY:

Complete the *Final Test* (RB pp. 138)

ART TO EXPLORE:
Texas Capitol 1882 by Elijah E. Myers
Treasured Artworks at the Capitol:
http://www.tfaoi.com/aa/1aa/1aa4.htm

SUGGESTED READING:
The Capitol Story: Statehouse in Texas by Mike Fowler and Jack Maguire (teens/adults)
Bluebonnet at the Texas State Capitol by Mary Brooke Casad
Capitols of Texas by Seymour Connor and others (Texian Press, 1970)
Lone Star Politics by Paul Benson and others (teens/adults)

Twenty Questions and Memory Game Suggestions:

Insert current names of . . .

Present Governor, present Lieutenant Governor, present Texas Attorney General, both present U.S. senators from Texas, your U.S. congressman/woman who represents you from Texas, your representative in the Texas House of Representatives, your senator in the Texas Senate

PLACES TO VISIT:

Texas Capitol – Austin (Be sure to take the free tour after entering the main doors. Take time to visit the chambers of both the Senate and House of Representatives, especially if they are in session. The grounds and its many statues also provide an enjoyable stroll.)

The Governor's Mansion: The Governor's Mansion is located within a short walking distance to the capitol. Tours are available, but reservations are required.
http://gov.texas.gov/mansion/tours

Texas State Cemetery - Austin

Your County Courthouse - Find your courthouse and enjoy all the different styles of architecture:
http://www.254texascourthouses.net/

Old postcards with Texas courthouses – has yours changed over time?
http://courthousehistory.com/gallery/states/texas

WRITING
PROMPT
PAGE 133

WEBSITES:

Texas State Preservation Board – Texas Capitol:
http://www.tspb.texas.gov/prop/tc/tc/capitol.html

Texas Government for Kids: http://kids.house.state.tx.us/

Old postcards with Texas courthouses – has yours changed over time?
http://courthousehistory.com/gallery/states/texas

Recipes

AWARD WINNING TEXAS CHILI

- Prep Time: 30 mins
- Total Time: 2 hrs
- Servings: 10-12

INGREDIENTS
* 2 1/2 lbs ground sirloin (or hamburger of your choice)
* 1 (14 ounce) can of beef broth
* 1/2 can chicken broth
* 1 (8 ounce) can of tomato sauce
* 2 teaspoons granulated or minced onion
* 3/4 teaspoon cayenne
* 2 teaspoons beef bouillon granules
* 1/4 teaspoon salt
* 2 teaspoons chicken bouillon granules
* 1-2 Tablespoons light chili powder
* 5 Tablespoons dark chili powder
* 3 teaspoons ground cumin
* 2 1/4 teaspoons granulated garlic or garlic powder
* 1/4 teaspoon brown sugar

DIRECTIONS
1. Brown ground sirloin and drain.
2. Add beef broth, chicken broth, and tomato sauce to meat and bring to a boil.
3. Add first spices: 2 tsp granulated onion, 1/2 tsp cayenne, 2 tsp beef granules, 1/4 tsp salt, 2 tsp chicken granules, 1 Tbsp light chili powder, 2 Tbsp dark chili powder.
4. Cover and cook 1 hour on low.
5. After 1 hour add: 2 tsp ground cumin, 2 tsp granulated garlic, 2 Tbsp dark chili powder, 1 Tbsp light chili powder. (Be sure to taste and decide whether to add more chili powder or not.)
6. Adjust liquid with remainder of chicken broth, if necessary.
7. Cover and cook 30 minutes.
8. Add: 1 Tbsp dark chili powder, 1 tsp ground cumin, 1/4 tsp granulated garlic, 1/4 tsp cayenne, 1/4 tsp brown sugar. (Again, make sure you can handle more chili powder!)
9. Reduce heat to a slow boil.
10. Cook 10 minutes.
11. Adjust salt, cayenne, and chili powder to taste.

KING RANCH CHICKEN CASSEROLE

INGREDIENTS:
* 1/2 cup chopped onion
* 1/2 cup chopped green bell pepper
* 1/4 cup butter
* 1 can condensed cream of mushroom soup
* 1 can condensed cream of chicken soup
* 1 can of tomatoes with green chilies (don't drain)
  or if you don't like spicy, just use a can of regular tomatoes (don't drain the tomatoes)
* 2 cups cooked chicken breast, chopped
* 12 corn tortillas (tear into bit-sized pieces)
* 2 cups cheddar cheese (shredded)

DIRECTIONS:
1. Preheat oven to 325° and grease a 13x9 casserole dish.
2. Melt the butter and saute onion and bell pepper till tender. Add both cans of soup and the can of tomatoes. Finally, add the chicken breast and mix all together.
3. Make three layers. First, put down layer of tortillas. On top of that, add a layer of the soup and chicken sauce. Top the sauce with shredded cheese. Do this three times, and be sure to divide the ingredients into thirds. Cheese will be on the very top.
4. Cook your casserole for about 45 minutes (uncovered) until it bubbles on top.

SPAETZLE (dumplings)

INGREDIENTS:
* 2 eggs (beaten)
* 1/4 cup milk
* 1 cup flour
* 1/2 teaspoon nutmeg
* dash salt and pepper
* 1-2 Tablespoons butter

DIRECTIONS:
1. Mix milk, beaten eggs, flour, salt/pepper, and nutmeg in a bowl.

2. Fill a large pot about half-way with water. Boil.

3. Once the water is boiling, push a few tablespoons of batter at a time through either a colander or a spaetzle maker. Carefully drop the dough into the boiling water and stir a few times. After about five minutes, the dough will rise to the top of the water and will be tender. Drain and toss with butter. (makes 3-4 servings)

SHRIMP GUMBO

INGREDIENTS:
* 1 cup chopped onion
* 1-2 cups green bell pepper, chopped
* 3 garlic cloves, minced
* 1/2 pound sausage (kielbasa or your favorite), slice longwise and then cut into 1/4 inch pieces
* 1(14 oz) can of diced tomatoes (don't drain)
* 1 bay leaf
* 1 can chicken broth
* 1/2 teaspoon chili powder
* salt/pepper to taste
* 3/4 pound uncooked shrimp (peel and devein first)
* 1/2 cup instant rice

DIRECTIONS:
1. Put a little oil or butter in a pan and saute the onion and garlic for a few minutes.
2. Add the sausage and cook till the sides begin to brown. Add bell pepper and cook for a few more minutes.
3. Add tomatoes, chicken broth, the bay leaf, and seasonings. Boil for another few minutes, then stir in the shrimp. Cook for 3-4 minutes until shrimp is pink.
4. Add the rice and take off the heat. Cover and let the pot sit for about 5 minutes (or until the rice is soft). Remove the bay leaf before eating.
Serves 4.
** This is an easy gumbo for your first try! You can find more difficult recipes that include okra and other ingredients your family might enjoy.

FRIJOLES (BEANS)

INGREDIENTS:
* 2 cups pinto beans (let's make these from scratch and not a can!)
* 1 onion, chopped
* a few cloves of minced garlic
* a few Tablespoons of chili powder (if you are brave!)
* salt/pepper
* optional: you can also add bacon and other meats to add flavor to the beans
1. Soak beans overnight. Drain and rinse the beans several times.
2. Add rest of ingredients and cook over medium heat until tender.
3. Serve with tortillas or cornbread.

THREE SISTERS SOUP

INGREDIENTS:
* 1 cup dried beans (soak overnight)
* 1 acorn squash
* 1 cup corn (canned, frozen, or cut off the cob)
* 1 onion
* 1 celery stalk (diced)
* 3-4 cups broth (chicken, beef, or vegetable)
* optional: garlic, salt, pepper, carrots

DIRECTIONS:
1. First, drain and rinse the beans which have been soaked overnight (or use canned beans). If using dried beans, cover with water and simmer about 45 minutes until tender.
2. Cut acorn squash in half; scoop out seeds. Bake each half of the squash (cut side up) for 45 minutes at 375° (they will be tender).
3. Saute the diced onion in a little butter or oil until it is soft.
4. Add garlic, celery, carrots, and other spices/salt/pepper to taste.
5. Scoop out the cooked squash. Either dice it or smooth out the lumps. Add to the onion mixture.
6. Rinse and drain the cooked beans.
7. Add the broth to the vegetable mixture and simmer for about 15 minutes, stirring occasionally. Enjoy!

VERMICELLI

INGREDIENTS:
*1 lb vermicelli noodles (or angel hair pasta)
* 4 cups chicken or beef broth
* 2 Tablespoons grated parmesan cheese

DIRECTIONS:
Boil pasta until al dente (that means until it is just a bit chewy - don't let it get too soft and mushy) in the broth. Scoop out and top with cheese and any other spices desired. Add salt and pepper to taste. Yummy!

FLOUR TORTILLAS

INGREDIENTS:
* 2 1/2 cups all-purpose flour
* 1 teaspoon baking powder
* 1 cup hot water
* pinch salt
* 1/4 cup butter or shortening

DIRECTIONS:
1. Mix flour, baking powder, and salt in mixing bowl. Add the butter or shortening with your fingers (this is the fun part!). Work the ingredients together until you can no longer see the butter.
2. Add a little less than 1 cup of hot water and mix it in with a fork. You might need to add a bit more water to make all the dough come together.
3. Sprinkle a little flour on the counter. Take the dough from the bowl and knead it about ten times. (the dough should be smooth). If it's too sticky, add a little more flour.
4. Divide the dough in half, then in half again, then in half again - you should have 8 pieces of dough now.
5. Let the dough sit, covered with a clean dish towel, for about 30 minutes.
6. Sprinkle flour on the counter, and roll out each piece of dough with a rolling pin into an 8-inch diameter circle.
7. Spray a pan with cooking spray or add a little butter to the skillet. Cook each tortilla for 30 seconds to one minute on each side. Be sure to wrap the cooked tortillas in a towel to keep them soft.
8. You can eat them plain. Spread a little butter on them. Fill with peanut butter and jelly and roll up. Make little burritos or tacos with meat and veggies. So many delicious combinations, so little time!

BUTTERMILK PIE

INGREDIENTS:
* 1 1/2 cup granulated sugar
* 3 Tablespoons all-purpose flour
* 1 cup buttermilk
* 3 eggs, beaten
* 1/4 cup melted butter
* 1 teaspoon vanilla extract
* dash of nutmeg
* 1/2 cup chopped pecans (optional)
* 9-inch pie pastry crust (make it fresh or buy it pre-made frozen)

DIRECTIONS:
1. Mix sugar, flour, buttermilk, and eggs (use a whisk).
2. Add melted butter, nutmeg, and vanilla.
3. Pour into pie crust and sprinkle pecans on top. Place pie on a cookie sheet so it's stable.
4. Bake at 350° for about 35 minutes (you might have to put a foil tent around the crust so it doesn't burn towards the end of baking time). It's ready when the center is almost firm - just a tiny bit jiggly.
5. Refrigerate.

PEANUT BRITTLE

*3 cups sugar
*2 cups water
*3/4 cup light corn syrup
*3/4 cup dark corn syrup
*3-4 cups coarsely chopped salted
  roasted peanuts
*2 Tablespoons (1/4 stick) unsalted butter
*1 Tablespoon baking soda
*1 teaspoon vanilla extract

DIRECTIONS:
1. Grease two baking sheets.
2. Heat first four ingredients until sugar dissolves.
3. Turn heat to high and boil until temperature reaches 260°F (it will take about 35-40 minutes).
4. Add the peanuts and butter and boil for approximately 15 minutes, until temperature is 295°F.
5. Stir in vanilla and baking soda quickly (it will foam).
6. Pour out immediately, dividing it in half between two baking sheets.
7. Cool, break into pieces, and store covered.

HARDTACK CRACKERS

INGREDIENTS:
* 2 cups flour
* pinch of salt
* 1/2 - 3/4 cups water

DIRECTIONS:
1. Stir together flour and salt in mixing bowl.
2. Add water and mix with hands until dough comes together.
3. Sprinkle some flour on the counter and roll out the dough until it's about 1/3 inch thick.
4. Cut dough into 3 x 3 inch squares. Use a chopstick or something else with a point and poke 16 evenly-spaced holes in each square. Place on a cookie sheet.
5. Bake 4 hours at 250°, turning over once halfway through baking time. Cool on rack.
** These crackers aren't like typical crackers. Just like their name implies, they are HARD! The best way to eat them is to soak them in water or let them sit in your mouth till they soften. You can also soften them in water a bit and then fry them (Civil War soldiers fried them in pork fat!).

JOHNNY CAKES

INGREDIENTS:
* 2 cups cornmeal
* 2/3 cup milk
* 2 Tablespoons oil
* 1 teaspoon baking soda
* 1/2 teaspoon salt

DIRECTIONS:
1. Mix ingredients together in bowl.
2. Divide dough into 8 "dodgers."
3. Bake at 350° for 20-25 minutes or fry the dodgers in hot cooking oil.
4. When cool, smear them with a little butter or molasses.

COPY WORK

UNIT 1: TEXAS STATE SYMBOLS

Copy the Texas Pledge:

> *Honor the Texas flag;*
> *I pledge allegiance to thee, Texas,*
> *One state under God,*
> *One and indivisible.*

UNIT 2: REGIONS OF TEXAS

Copy and illustrate the famous Sam Houston quote:

> *"Texas is the finest portion of the globe that has ever blessed my vision."*
>
> -Sam Houston, from a letter written to John H. Houston, July 31, 1833

UNIT 3: NATIVE AMERICANS OF TEXAS

Copy this entry by a chronicler of the Coronado expedition:

> *"They dry the flesh in the sun, and make a sort of soup of it to eat. A handful thrown into a pot swells up so as to increase very much. They season it with fat, which they always try to secure when they kill a cow."* - Excerpt from *The Coronado Expedition: 1540-42* by George Parker Winship. Washington: The U.S. Bureau of American Ethology, 1896.

(Tonkawa) Copy and illustrate this old Cherokee legend:

> *A grandfather sat down with his grandson one evening around the fire. He explained to the boy that a battle goes on inside all people.*
>
> *"My son, there is a battle between two 'wolves' inside us all," he said. "One wolf is Evil. It is anger, envy, jealousy, sorrow, regret, greed, arrogance, self-pity, guilt, resentment, lies, false pride, superiority, and ego.*
>
> *"The other wolf is Good. It is joy, peace, love, hope, humility, kindness, empathy, generosity, truth, and faith."*
>
> *After thinking quietly for a time, the boy looked at the grandfather and asked, "Which wolf wins the battle?"*
>
> *The old Cherokee smiled at the boy. "The one you feed," he replied.*

Copy and illustrate this short excerpt from the poem "The Corsair":

> *O'er the glad waters of the dark blue sea,*
> *Our thoughts as boundless, and our souls as free,*
> *Far as the breeze can bear, the billows foam,*
> *Survey our empire and behold our home!*
> - Excerpt from "The Corsair" by Lord Byron (1814)

First, copy the proper and complete name of the Mexican Constitution in English, and then rewrite the name of the Constitution in Spanish:

> **English:** *The Federal Constitution of the United Mexican States of 1824*
> **Spanish:** *Constitución Federal de los Estados Unidos Mexicanos de 1824*

Copy Mary Austin Holley's description of Texas, then illustrate:

> *The surface is beautifully, and often fancifully diversified with prairie and woodland; presenting to the enterprising farmer, large and fertile fields already cleared by the hand of nature, and waiting, as it were, to receive the plough.*
> -Mary Austin Holley, from her book *Texas* (1831)

UNIT 6: REVOLUTION!

Copy this paragraph that relates to the issues caused by living at such a great distance from the state capital:

> *Coahuila being so far distant from the population of Texas, and so widely variant from it in interests, the rights and wants of the people of Texas cannot be properly protected and provided for, under the present organization, admitting the several Departments of the Government of the State to be prompted by the utmost purity of intention, in their efforts for the administration of justice. Coahuila and Texas are dissimilar in soil, climate and productions, in common interests, and partly in population.*
> -Excerpt from *The History of Texas* by David B. Edward (1836)

Copy Austin's prison diary entry from February 22, 1834. Illustrate:

> *What a horrible punishment is solitary confinement, shut up in a dungeon with scarcely light to distinguish anything. If I were a criminal it would be one thing, But I am not one. I have been ensnared and precipitated, but my intentions were pure and correct."*
> -Excerpt from "The Prison Journal of Stephen F. Austin" *The Quarterly of the Texas State Historical Association* Vol. 2, No. 3 (Jan., 1899), pp. 183-210.

Copy the first three articles from the public version of the *Treaty of Velasco*:

Article 1st: General Antonio López de Santa Anna agrees that he will not take up arms, nor will he exercise his influence to cause them to be taken up against the people of Texas, during the present war of Independence.
Article 2nd: All hostilities between the Mexican and Texian troops will cease immediately both on land and water.
Article 3rd: The Mexican troops will evacuate the Territory of Texas, passing to the other side of the Rio Grande del Norte.

UNIT 7: THE REPUBLIC OF TEXAS

Copy this account and then illustrate a funny story in Texas history:

"Houston, knowing something of Lamar's nervousness, took occasion to make an exaugural, reviewing at great length his administration and by the time he was done, Lamar had become so nervous that he could not read his inaugural, and had to commit it to his private secretary, Algernon Thompson, to be read to an exhausted audience."
-Excerpt from "Allen's Reminiscences of Texas 1838-42" in the Southwestern Historical Quarterly, *Texas State Historical Association*, volume 18 (1915), p. 295.

Copy this brief section of the address:

Perhaps no government on earth combines freedom and security in a more eminent degree than that which we have established. It circumscribes the liberty of none; but leaves every individual to pursue happiness in his own way with no other restrictions on his conduct than such as are essential to the maintenance of justice and the preservation of the public morals.
-Mirabeau Lamar, *Address to the People of Santa Fe,* June 5, 1841

UNIT 8: STATEHOOD

Copy General Granger's proclamation that slaves were now free, given on the first "Juneteenth" in 1865 in Galveston.

"The people of Texas are informed that in accordance with a Proclamation from the Executive of the United States, all slaves are free. This involves an absolute equality of rights and rights of property between former masters and slaves, and the connection heretofore existing between them becomes that between employer and free laborer."
-Major General Gordon Granger, Galveston, June 19th, 1865

Copy this portion of the John H. Reagan letter from prison (August 11, 1865) as you imagine sitting in a dark cell, perhaps the only light coming from a candle or a small window:

> *"To the People of Texas: . . . I take the liberty of suggesting to you . . . to accept the present condition of things, as the result of war. . . The State occupies the condition of a conquered nation. State government and State sovereignty are in abeyance, and will be so until you adopt a government and policy acceptable to the conquerors. A refusal to accede to these conditions would only result in prolongation of the time during which you will be deprived of a civil government of your own choice."*
>
> -Memoirs With Special References to Secession and the Civil War by John H. Reagan, New York and Washington: The Neale Publishing Co, 1906, pp. 290-92.

UNIT 9: COWBOYS AND INDIANS

In 1889, Dagmar Mariager participated in a buffalo hunt. Copy the beautiful language he uses to describe his first encounter with the buffalo, up close.

> *Nothing but the deep breathing and the grinding of the ponderous jaws broke the stillness of the fog surrounding us. I felt that I must sink into the earth for safety. I wanted to scream, but dared not.*
>
> -The Overland Monthly and Out West Magazine, Volume 14, Issue 80, August 1889, pp. 190-196. (University of Michigan Library collections)

UNIT 10: TEXAS IN THE 20TH CENTURY

Copy this short exerpt from a real World War II Texas soldier's letter home to his wife. This particular soldier was based in the Philippines during the war. He decorated the front of almost every envelope he sent home with animals and plants from the islands where he was stationed.

> *21 March 1945*
> *My windfall finally came again! Four letters from you! Your writing about picking the first hyacinths makes me all the more homesick. I would never want to live in the tropics and have to miss the changes of the seasons. We listen to the radio religiously every night, hoping to hear that German organized resistance has collapsed. It will have such a bearing on speeding up the defeat of Japan. Some new officers are arriving fresh from the States again, and I'm beginning to feel like an old timer until I think about the ones still here after 30 months or more in this theater.*
> *Many much love, ole Funny Thing ...*

*We have provided a more comprehensive list of sources for these copy work excerpts at the end of the bibliography section.

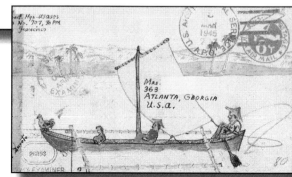

ANSWER KEYS

Unit Tests

Unit One: Texas State Symbols
1. F   2. T   3. F   4. F   5. T   6. D   7. E   8. C   9. C   10. C
11. symbol   12. diverse   13. perpendicular   14. horizontal   15. affixed
<u>Honor</u>, <u>flag</u>, <u>allegiance</u>, <u>Texas</u>, <u>state</u>, <u>indivisible</u>
Mockingbird, Longhorn, Bluebonnet, Pecan, Rodeo, Chili, Blue Topaz, Guadalupe Bass

Unit Two: Regions of Texas
1. F   2. T   3. F   4. T   5. F   6. B   7. E   8. C   9. A   10. D
11. delta   12. reservoirs   13. inhabitants   14. aquifer   15. estuaries

7 - Playa Lakes	6 - Aerospace	1 - Citrus fruits	5 - State Capitol	6 - Barrier Islands
1 - Subtropical	7 - Amarillo	3 - Desert	7 - Wind Power Production	
2 - Dallas	4 - Timber	5 - Granite	3 - Guadalupe Mountain	

Unit Three: Native Americans of Texas
1. T   2. F   3. T   4. F   5. F   6. C   7. B   8. A   9. D   10. E
11. pemmican   12. shaman   13. tanning   14. quiver   15. adobe
Caddos 4   Karankawa 6   Coahuiltecans 1, 5, 6   Comanche 2, 5, 7   Tonkawa 2, 5, 6
Apache 1, 3, 5, 7   Jumano 1, 3, 5   Tigua 3

Unit Four: Explorers and Missionaries
1. F   2. F   3. T   4. T   5. T   6. B   7. A   8. C   9. B   10. D
11. presidio   12. convert   13. turquoise   14. allies   15. friars

1.	Explorer - F	8.	Captain - C
2.	Conquistador - J	9.	Settler - L
3.	Emperor - N	10.	Convert - D
4.	Sailor - A	11.	Clergy - E
5.	Slave - B	12.	Bishop - H
6.	Viceroy - G	13.	Soldier - K
7.	Friar - M	14.	Missionary - I

Unit Five: Filibusters and Empressarios
1. T   2. T   3. F   4. T   5. F   6. C   7. C   8. B   9. B   10. D
11. infamous   12. strife   13. republican   14. social change   15. royalists

Unit Six: Revolution!
1. T   2. T   3. T   4. T   5. F   6. C   7. A   8. B   9. D   10. D
11. halted   12. arms   13. dictator   14. disloyal   15. reinforcements

Order of Events:
Texas no longer governed by Spain, Old 300 move to Texas, Convention of 1832, Austin travels to Mexico to meet with Santa Anna, Come and Take It, Battle of the Alamo, Runaway Scrape, Loss at Goliad, Battle of San Jacinto

Unit Seven: The Republic of Texas
1. F   2. T   3. F   4. F   5. T   6. D   7. A   8. B   9. C   10. D
11. furloughed   12. imported   13. consecutive   14. representatives   15. archives

Unit Eight: Statehood and Civil War
1. T   2. F   3. F   4. F   5. T   6. B   7. C   8. A   9. D   10. C
11. joint resolution   12. simple majority   13. ceded   14. alleviated   15. impeached
North or South:
1. S 2. S 3. N 4. N 5. S 6. N 7. N 8. S 9. N 10. S 11. S 12. S 13. N 14. S 15. S 16. N

Unit Nine: Cowboys and Indians
1. F   2. F   3. T   4. F   5. T   6. B   7. A   8. D   9. B   10. C
11. tenant farmers   12. vaqueros   13. tallow   14. stockyards   15. plantations

Unit Ten: Texas in the 20th Century
1. F   2. T   3. T   4. F   5. T   6. B   7. A   8. D   9. B   10. B
11. seawall   12. animals   13. Franklin Rooselvelt   14. France   15. chip

Unit Eleven: Texas Government Today
1. F   2. F   3. F   4. F   5. T   6. B   7. C   8. B   9. D   10. A
11. judicial   12. civil   13. Texas   14. cities   15. school district

UNIT ONE: SYMBOLS

Texas Flag: Senator William Wharton

State Song: Alaska was annexed to the United States and became the largest state in the U.S.A.

Other State Symbols: Pan de Campo (or Cowboy Bread)

UNIT TWO: REGIONS OF TEXAS

South Texas Plains: Running W brand

Prairies and Lakes: River of the Arms of God

Piney Woods: Sam Houston State University

Hill Country: Bedrock mortars are spots in rock where prehistoric people pounded their food.

Gulf Coast: It is a 1,300-mile inland waterway (man-made canal) running from Brownsville, Texas, to St. Marks, Florida, along the Gulf of Mexico coastline.

Native Plants and Animals: Dasypus novemcinctus – 9 hinged bands of bony plates

UNIT THREE: NATIVE AMERICANS OF TEXAS

Origins: Depending on where you start in Alaska, your answer should be over 4,000 miles.

Early Prehistoric Indians: Flint

Buffalo: Up to 40 miles per hour

HISTORIC INDIANS

Karankawa: Kaktos translates to spiny plant or thistle.

Coahuiltecan: The spines can be burned off and/or the skin of the prickly pear carefully peeled away from the tasty fruit. Some animals eat the fruit, thorns and all, and some suffer mouth wounds from which they might never recover. That's why the fruit has thorns—to protect the plant and seeds from being eaten. The old Texas longhorns were usually tough enough to handle the thorns, but other types of cattle introduced later were not.

Comanche: If you follow all the little meanderings of the boundary rivers and coastline, the perimeter of Texas measures about 3,800 miles. If he walked 3 miles per hour, it would take him 1,267 hours (or about 53 days).

Tonkawa: The Texas Rangers

Lipan and Kiowa Apaches: Average 25 pounds per hive annually

Jumano: 1,885 miles long

Tigua: Eli Whitney invented the cotton gin.

UNIT FOUR: EXPLORERS AND MISSIONARIES

Timeline of World Exploration: 24,874 miles around the equator.

Spanish Explorers: The Texas coastline is 367 miles long. (If you include tidal inlets = 3,359 miles long.)

Missions and Presidios: 1849; "garrisoned place"

UNIT FIVE: FILIBUSTERS AND EMPRESARIOS

Filibusters: He partnered with Jean Lafitte in a slave-running business.

Mexico Overthrows the Spanish Empire: President of the United States of Mexico (Estados Unidos Mexicanos).

Moses Austin: The Baron de Bastrop

Stephen F. Austin: No

Other Empresarios: Between the Guadalupe and Colorado Rivers and in the northeast area of Texas on the Red River (with Arthur G. Wavell)

UNIT 6: REVOLUTION

Trouble at Anahuac: translates as "land on the edge of the water" and was the name of the heartland of Aztec Mexico.

Battle of Velasco: Surfside Beach (Freeport)

Santa Anna: His leg!

Austin's Trip to Mexico: Father Michael Muldoon, an Irish priest he knew from Texas, brought reading material to Austin.

Battle of Gonzales: colonist Ezekiel Williams

March to Goliad and San Antonio: The distance is about 3 miles between Mission Concepción and the Alamo.

Texians Fight Their Way Into San Antonio: Veramendi House (Jim Bowie was married to a Veramendi daughter.)

UNIT SEVEN: THE REPUBLIC OF TEXAS

A New Country Begins: 1.25 million-dollar debt inherited after the revolution; U.S. national debt at the time of this book's publication was close to 20 trillion dollars. You can check the current balance of the debt here: **http://www.usdebtclock.org/**

First Things First: At the time of this writing, a Subway Sandwich shop.

Mirabeau Lamar: David G. Burnet served as vice president under Lamar.

Sam Houston's Second Term: Margaret Lea Houston; they had eight children.

The Mier Expedition: They escaped through a tunnel and from a hole bored through the walls.

UNIT EIGHT: STATEHOOD

Texas Joins the U.S.: President John Tyler

Mexican-American War: Taylor became the 12th President of the United States.

Trouble Brewing: 14.4 pounds

The Battle For Galveston: They belonged to the Confederacy.

The Civil War is Over: January 1, 1863 (officially issued) – June 19, 1865

Reconstruction: Except as punishment for a crime (after conviction)

Texas After Reconstruction: Established by Governor Davis, the so-called "obnoxious acts" allowed the governor the power to declare martial law to maintain order in the state.

UNIT NINE: COWBOYS AND INDIANS

The Plains Indians Attack: Quanah Parker

Native Americans on the Rio Grande: They were expected to fight Indians during times of trouble and protect cattle herds and settlers. They were also known to escort and protect trains and stagecoaches.

Farming: a raw material or agricultural product

Change and Progress: oil for frying food, an insecticide, an ingredient in creams and lotions

UNIT TEN: TEXAS IN THE TWENTIETH CENTURY

Where do Oil and Gas Come From: Uranium is not a fossil fuel. It is a radioactive element which is converted into a fuel at nuclear power plants.

Texas Following World War I: Foreign Secretary Arthur Zimmerman

Texas After World War II: It was a 1965 initiative supported by President Johnson to improve the appearance near interstate highways through control of outdoor advertising, screening or removal of certain junkyards within sight of the highways, and promotion of roadside development and scenic improvements.

Texas and the Cold War: This changes frequently, so you can check for the today's price here:
http://www.nasdaq.com/markets/crude-oil.aspx

UNIT ELEVEN: TEXAS GOVERNMENT

Who We are and Where We Live: Check current populations for Los Ybanez and Houston (the smallest and largest cities at the time of this printing).

ANSWERS TO OTHER ACTIVITY QUESTIONS ...

Unit One: Symbols

•**OTHER TEXAS SYMBOLS - COMPILING DATA:** Cobbler-Peach, Crustacean-Gulf Coast Shrimp, Dog Breed-Blue Lacy, Footwear-Cowboy Boots, Fruit-Ruby Red Grapefruit, Hat-Cowboy Hat, Musical Instrument-Guitar, Pastries-sopaipilla and strudel, Shrub-Crape Myrtle, Snack-Tortilla Chips and Salsa, Vegetable-Texas Sweet Onion, and Vehicle-Chuck Wagon.

Unit Two: Regions of Texas

•**ON THE ROAD AGAIN:** Houston to Huntsville=70.4 miles; Huntsville to Centerville=49 miles; Centerville to Ennis=89 miles; Ennis to Fort Worth=57.4 miles; Fort Worth to Waco=90 miles; Waco to Austin;102.3 miles; Austin to San Antonio=79.4 miles

Total number of miles traveled: 537.5 miles

(Distances taken from a computerized mapping program and may not match student's answers exactly.)

•**WHAT'S MY NAME RIDDLES:**

1. South America   2. Europe   3. Arctic Ocean   4. Indian Ocean   5. North America 6. Australia
7. Pacific Ocean   8. Oregon   9. Alabama   10. Texas   11. Lubbock 12. Houston

•**LATITUDE AND LONGITUDE BINGO:**

Oregon: 45° N, 120° W; Idaho: 45° N, 115° W; South Dakota: 45° N, 100° W; Minnesota: 45° N, 95° W
Wisconsin: 45° N, 90° W; Michigan: 45° N, 85° W; Maine: 45° N, 70° W; Nevada: 40° N, 115° W
Utah: 40° N, 110° W; Colorado: 40° N, 105° W; Missouri: 40° N, 95° W; Illinois: 40° N, 90° W
Indiana: 40° N, 85° W; Pennsylvania: 40° N, 80° W; North Carolina: 35° N, 80° W;
Oklahoma: 35°N, 95° W; Pacific Ocean: 30° N, 120° W; New Mexico: 35° N, 105° W;
Arizona: 35° N, 110° W; California: 35° N, 120° W; Atlantic Ocean: 30° N, 75° W;
Texas: 30° N, 100° W; Louisiana: 30° N, 90° W; Florida: 30° N, 85° W

• **SORTING TEXAS REGIONS (ACCEPTABLE ANSWERS):**

Big Bend Country: mountains, driest part of the state, El Paso, oil & gas, fewest cities, ranching, rugged plateaus; *Hill Country*: granite quarries, caverns & springs, State Capitol, the Alamo, oil & gas, cattle, San Antonio; *Gulf Coast:* estuaries, petrochemicals & aerospace, cattle, Rio Grande Delta, oil & gas; *Piney Woods*: swamps & wetlands, greatest rainfall, lumber, cattle, oil & gas; *Panhandle Plains:* playa lakes, ranching, oil & gas, flat & treeless, wind power; *Prairies & Lakes*: tall grasses, fertile black soil, Trinity, Brazos & Red Rivers, Dinosaur State Park, cattle, oil & gas, aircraft building, Dallas; *South TX Plains:* sub-tropical climate, oil & gas, cattle, citrus trees

• **MAP VOCABULARY QUIZ:**

1. G   2. J   3. B   4. E   5. F   6. I   7. A   8. D   9. K   10. L   11. C   12. H

Unit Three: Native Americans of Texas

•**BUFFALO - ECONOMICS:** The buffalo nickel was minted between 1913-1938, but the design was changed because the dates wore off easily. Five cents in 1920 would be equivalent to the buying power of 64 cents today.

•**COMANCHE - MATH:** The average walking speed is 3 mph, the average jogging speed of a horse is 10 mph, the average driving speed of a car is 50 mph, and the farthest distance across Texas is approximately 800 miles. If you traveled *non-stop* (no sleep, food, or potty breaks!) it would take:

Walking: 266 hours (11 days)

Horse: 80 hours (3 days)

Car: 16 hours (less than 1 day)

•**TONKAWA - SCIENCE:** Gray wolves no longer live in the wild in Texas. They are considered endangered, but their level of protection varies in the states where they still exist. Including in Alaska, there are approximately 16,000 gray wolves in the U.S. today.

•**JUMANO - GEOGRAPHY:** The mileage from Agreda, Spain, to El Paso, Texas (or you might have calculated to a different spot), is approximately 5,450 miles. If the average walking speed is 3 mph, the average biking speed is 10 mph, and an average airplane flies at 500 mph, and if you traveled *non-stop* it would take:

Walking: 1816 hours (about 75 days)

Bike: 545 hours (22 days)

Plane: 11 hours (1/2 a day)

•**OTHER TRIBES - MATH:**

Columbus Visits New World (1492) and Battle of the Alamo (1836) = 344 years

Coronado's Expedition Begins (1540) and Spindletop Gusher (1901) = 361 years

Pineda Maps the Gulf (1519) and Sam Houston Elected Governor of Texas (1859) = 340 years

Great Galveston Hurricane (1900) and Man Lands on the Moon (1969) = 69 years

Unit Four: Explorers and Missionaries

•**EXAMPLE OF WORDS TO USE A TO Z CHART-EXPLORERS AND MISSIONARIES**

A: astrolabe (compass), Asia (trade for jewels, gold, silk & spices), Aztec (fierce fighters)

B: blame (French settlers blamed La Salle for everything that went wrong)

C: caravel, convert (change belief), colony (settlement ruled by another country)

D: decade (10 years), drought (no rain)

E: expedition (journey made for a special reason), empire (group of many conquered places)

F: French (came to Texas in 1685), fish (common dinner with maize at the missions)

G: gold (explorers came to North America in search of it), Galveston (Cabeza de Vaca lived here with the Karankawas)

H: historical map (info from the past), heritage (way of life, customs & beliefs from past to today)

I: irrigation system (part of the watering plan for the city of San Antonio de Béxar)

J: *Just* an empty space

K: Karankawas (enslaved Spanish survivors)

L: legends (stories handed down over time), La Salle (sailed down the Mississippi)

M: missions (religious settlements), missionaries (priests who teach), Mestizos (Spanish plus Indian)

N: Niña, Pinta & Santa Maria (Columbus's ships), Narváez

O: Oñate (El Paso)

P: Portugese (1st to search for sea routes to Asia), presidio (fort), plaza (town square)

Q: Queen Isabella & King Ferdinand (gave money and boats to Columbus)

R: route (Europe to Asia), resist (act against), revolt (action against the people in charge)

S: San Salvador (where Columbus landed), self-sufficient (able to make everything needed)

T: trade (made men rich & powerful), timeline

U: *unfilled* box

V: Vespucci (found Brazil), vaqueros (cowboys)

W: West Europeans (sailed west to find Asia)

X: *Xtremely* empty box

Y: Ysleta (fist mission)

Z: Zuni Indians (killed Esteban)

•**TIMELINE OF WORLD EXPLORATION - WRITING:**

Century (centum) = 100 years, millennia (mille) = 1,000 years, decade (decas) = 10 years

Columbus discovered the New World five centuries and two decades (plus a few years) ago.

•**MAJOR MISSIONS OF TEXAS:** *Big Bend* (Mission Ysleta, Mission Socorro); *Piney Woods* (San Fransisco de los Tejas, Nuestra Señora de los Dolores); *South Tx Plains/Gulf Coast* (Mission La Bahía/Goliad, Nuestra Señora del Refugio); *Hill Country* (Mission Espada, San Juan Capistrano, Mission Concepción, Alamo/San Antonio de Valero, Mission San José, San Sabá Mission)

•**MISSIONS AND PRESIDIOS - MATH/ECONOMICS:** The population of the world today is approximately 7 billion people. 7 billion times 4.85 bushels = 33,950,000,000 (almost 34 billion bushels!). Current cost of 1 bushel of corn = $3.70 each (that's about 70 pounds of corn, if it's still on the ear).

Unit Five: Filibusters and Empresarios

•**EMPRESARIOS - MATH:** It is about 900 miles from Herculaneum, Missouri, to San Antonio, Texas. Of course the number of gallons your car might use depends on the type of car you drive, how fast you drive, and other factors. However, if the cost of gas is $2.00 per gallon, and your car averages about 30 miles per gallon, you might use about 30 gallons of gas (30 miles per gallon x 30 gallons = 900 miles). In that case, your cost per mile would be close to .06 cents, and the total gas cost (one way) would be about $60.

•**OTHER EMPRESARIOS - MATH:** 1 League = 4.428 acres. 1 Labor = 177 acres, 1 Acre = 43,560 sq ft

Unit Six: Revolution!

•**CONVENTIONS OF 1832 AND 1833 - MATH:** San Felipe to Saltillo, MX = 495 miles, San Felipe to Monclova, MX = 441 miles, San Felipe to Mexico City = 1,007 miles, San Felipe to Austin = 117 miles, Austin, Tx, to Washington, D.C. = 1,523 miles

BATTLE OF GONZALES - MATH: Ratio of Texians to Mexican soldados at Gonzales = 150:100 or 15:10, or 3:2

•**MARCH TO GOLIAD AND SAN ANTONIO - SCIENCE:** They weigh the same. A pound is a pound! However, a pound of gold would have greater density and a pound of grass would have greater volume. (We realize gold is usually weighed in troy ounces, but this question is just for fun!)

•**THE RUNAWAY SCRAPE - MATH:** Andrade was left in charge of Béxar with 1,000 troops, but since he did not lead one of the three divisions, we won't count him. Gaona commanded 700 soldados, Urrea commanded over 1,300 men, and Santa Anna and Sesma led another 1,400. That's a total of 3,400 soldados on the march.

Gaona/total troops = 700/3400 = 7:34   Urrea/total troops = 1,300/3,400 = 13:34

Sesma & Santa Anna/total troops = 1.400/3,400 = 14: 34 = 7:17

•**THE RUNAWAY SCRAPE - GEOGRAPHY:** Santa Anna's troops marched about 250 miles with a route a bit straighter than Houston's. Although Houston started in Gonzales, which is closer to San Jacinto than San Antonio, he took a less direct route, resulting in about the same number of miles marched as his enemy, Santa Anna.

•**JUAN SEGUÍN:** 1. Béxar 2. Tejano 3. ally 4. colony 5. dominated 6. militia 7. resistance 8. courier 9. San Jacinto 10. withdrawal 11. elected 12. traitor 13. resign 14. apprehended 15. politics 16. Democratic 17. Seguin

I have Santa Anna: Who has the name of the Alamo leader who sent letters asking for help?

I have William B. Travis: Who has the Texian scout who burned Vince's Bridge?

I have Deaf Smith: Who has the man who took over for his father in bringing the Old 300 to Texas?

I have Stephen F. Austin: Who led his men into battle saying, "Who will go with old ___ ___ into San Antonio?"

I have Ben Milam: Who was advised to destroy the Alamo, but chose not to?

I have Jim Bowie: Who was the Mexican General in charge of the Massacre at Goliad?

I have Urrea: Who played his fiddle at the Alamo to keep up the spirits of the Texians?

I have Davy Crockett: Who was the leader of the Texas Army?

I have Sam Houston: Who has the woman who survived the Battle of the Alamo and was sent to deliver the news?

I have Susannah Dickinson: Who has the leader of the Texian troops at Goliad?

I have James Fannin: Who was the leader of the entire Mexican Army and Mexico?

Unit 7: The Republic of Texas

• FIRST THINGS FIRST - MATH: The ratio was 1:1 (13 slave states and 13 free states)

• THE MIER EXPEDITION - MATH: The ratio of black beans to white beans was 17:159. The ratio of black beans to the total number of beans was 17:176. The ratio of white beans to the total number of beans was 159:176. The number of prisoners spared execution was 159.

Unit 8: Statehood and the Civil War

•TEXAS JOINS THE USA - MATH: Austin to Washington, D.C. = 1,523 miles.
By horse (10 mph at a jog): 152 hours travel time. By train (about 50 mph): about 30 hours travel time. By car today (about 65 mph): about 23 hours. By plane: about 3 hours.

Unit 9: Cowboys and Indians

•MATH: Calculating hay needed for cows: 1,000 cow = 20 lbs of hay, 1,200 lb cow = 24 lbs of hay, 1,700 lb cow = 34 lbs of hay.

Unit Ten: Texas in the Twentieth Century

•ANSWER KEY *(ORDER OF CARDS)* FOR I HAVE, WHO HAS: FAMOUS PEOPLE OF THE 20TH CENTURY

I have Anthony Lucas: Who has the Texas governor who signed the bill giving women the right to vote in primaries?

I have William P. Hobby: Who has the president who requested Congress declare war on Germany in 1917?

I have Woodrow Wilson: Who has the heir to the throne of Austria-Hungary?

I have Archduke Ferdinand: Who has the president when the stock market crashed?

I have Herbert Hoover: Who has the dictator of Germany during WWII?

I have Adolph Hitler: Who has the pilot who earned more medals than any other American in WWII?

I have Audie Murphy: Who has the woman who served twice as governor of Texas?

I have Miriam "Ma" Ferguson: Who has the WWII Texan hero who later became president?

I have Dwight D. Eisenhower: Who has the president's wife who wanted to keep America beautiful?

I have Lady Bird Johnson: Who has the famous Texas heart surgeon?

I have Michael DeBakey: Who has the president who wanted a man on the moon by 1970?

I have John F. Kennedy: Who has the retired Justice of the Supreme Court?

I have Sandra Day O'Connor: Who has the 41ˢᵗ President of the United States?

I have George H.W. Bush: Who has the president who created the New Deal?

I have Franklin D. Roosevelt: Who has the woman who commanded the Women's Army Corps?

I have Oveta Culp Hobby: Who has the man whose father was also president?

I have George W. Bush: Who has the man who was in charge of drilling at Spindletop?

Unit Eleven: Texas Government Today

•**LEVELS OF GOVERNMENT**

National: prints and coins money, taxes the income of citizens, grants patents and copyrights, builds roads and highways, makes treaties, declares war

State: builds public schools and universities, issues licenses to professionals, builds roads and highways, issues marriage licenses, collects sales tax, issues licenses to drivers

Local: builds public parks and playgrounds, maintains fire departments, collects garbage, collects property taxes, maintains a police force

Early Explorers to the New World

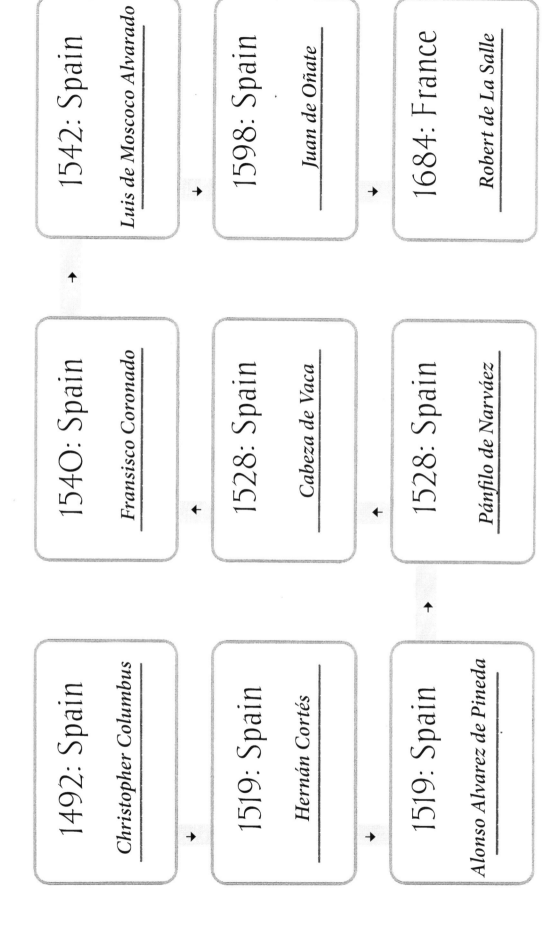

1492: Spain
Christopher Columbus

1519: Spain
Hernán Cortés

1519: Spain
Alonso Alvarez de Pineda

1540: Spain
Fransisco Coronado

1528: Spain
Cabeza de Vaca

1528: Spain
Pánfilo de Narváez

1542: Spain
Luis de Moscoco Alvarado

1598: Spain
Juan de Oñate

1684: France
Robert de La Salle

Houston vs. Lamar

SAM HOUSTON		MIRABEAU LAMAR
1836-38 1841-44	**Dates in office**	1838-41
1. Mirabeau Lamar 2. Edward Burleson	**Vice President**	David Burnet
1.25 million in 1836 Printed paper money/ inflation Collected taxes Reduced size of government	**Debt**	Issued more paper money Redbacks - more inflation End of term - $5 million in debt
Peace treaties	**Indians**	Disliked and wanted Indians removed; Battle of Neches; Council House Fight; Battle of Plum Creek
Archives War Mexican invasion Mier Expedition	**Mexico**	Built up navy Santa Fe Expedition

Lack of order

Had to write new constitution and elect officials

Land Policy

Sold and gave away land
Homestead Law

Slavery

Slavery legal

Military Protection

1836 placed army on leave
1841 reduced army and tried
to sell the navy

New Capital

Moved capital near Waterloo
and named it Austin
Too far from inland cities
Dislike for Houston

Education

Set aside land in each county
for public education
Set aside land for two
universities

North vs. South

Answer Key

President	*Abraham Lincoln*	*Jefferson Davis*
Commanding General	*Ulysses S. Grant*	*Robert E. Lee*
# of states	*24*	*11*
Capital City	*Washington, D.C.*	*Richmond, VA*
Associated Color	*Blue*	*Gray*
Nickname(s)	*Union*	*Confederacy/Rebels*
Flag	*Stars and Stripes*	*Stars and Bars*
Climate/ Geography	*Warm summers Cold winters Forests, bays, rivers*	*Warm summers Mild winters Rich fertile soil*
Population	*22 million*	*9.5 million (3.5 million were slaves)*
Cities	*Centers of trade and commerce Many large cities*	*Few cities Plantations: center of trade*
Economy	*Manufacturing Finances*	*Agriculture*
Culture	*Organized religion Public education*	*Traditional Conservative*
Transportation	*Railroads Good roads*	*Steamships Few railroads*
Military	*Strong navy*	*Small navy Good military leaders*
Other Factors	*Many factories produced war supplies Good telegraph system*	*Fighting on own soil with desire to win Shortage of war supplies*

Writing Prompts

Put on your author's hat! We'll start the story, then it's your job to finish it. Be creative!

Unit 1: Texas Symbols

Lizzie gently picked up the tiny Texas Horned Lizard.

"He's so small. I'll just hide him under my bed in a shoebox. Mom will never know," she plotted.

The next morning, Lizzie woke up. She looked under the bed and gasped . . .

The entire Brody family was exhausted. They had been driving all day from their old home in the Piney Woods, to their new home in the Panhandle Plains. Mr. Brody had recently accepted a job as Chief of Police in a small town near Lubbock.

Would they ever reach their destination?

"Stop!" cried Matt. "Check out those cotton fields! Let's take a close-up look!"

Mr. Brody slowed the car to a stop and everyone disembarked and stretched their weary arms and legs. Mrs. Brody stooped down to touch a soft cotton boll. As she rolled the fibers between her fingers, she let out a little yelp.

"Oh my! Look at this!"

They couldn't believe their eyes . . .

"Why do we have to do this?"

Slap. Slap.

"The mosquitoes! Someone has to do it!"

Slap. Slap.

"Oh, fine. But maybe first, we should . . . "

He opened his eyes slowly. His mouth felt dry and salty as he licked his lips. The sand was soft and still, unlike the rolling waves of the storm he and his men battled in the gulf.

He called out, but no answer.

Then he felt it. A cold, wet foot on his back. He twisted his head and saw . . .

All the way from Tennessee, through rain and mud. Terrible roads, if you could even call them roads. But we had finally arrived at our destination.

San Felipe de Austin.

"Hello? Mr. Austin? Anybody here?" my dad called.

We heard footsteps behind us. But it wasn't Mr. Austin . . .

Every year our family loves to attend the San Jacinto Festival. My favorite part is the reenactment. Actors dress up as Texian soldiers and Mexican soldados. Even Sam Houston and Santa Anna make an appearance!

The weather had been crazy all day. Sunny one moment, misty the next. As we found our spot, the actors took their places.

Suddenly, the mist rolled in again. The crowd moaned. Then . . . silence. As the fog lifted, I looked to my left and my right. The crowd had disappeared. I looked toward the huge obelisk monument. It was gone. The street was gone. The Battleship Texas was gone. Everything was gone.

Everything, that is, except a line of soldiers, quietly making their way across the field of tall grass.

Someone tapped my shoulder . . .

They pulled and pulled and pulled.

Everyone always says, "He's as strong as an ox." Now I know what they mean. But I never imagined they could pull something as large as this . . .

He was just a little boy. His dad and big brother were gone, off to defend Galveston. War was hard on everyone. His mother was sick; the one remaining horse was lame.

Someone had to plow the fields and plant the seed. He had seen his father do it plenty of times. He could do it, too.

The plow came to a complete stop. He could push no further. He reached down, assuming a large rock must be buried beneath the soil

He picked up the object, eyes wide, knowing their lives would never be the same.

She was his favorite cow. He greeted her each day, calling her by name. She would almost run to him, knowing he had an extra alfalfa cube for her in his pocket.

But, today was different . . .

"Oh great. I told you to bring a map!"

"I told you to bring your cell phone! Now look at us! Lost! I have no idea where we are."

The two sat in silence, waiting for the other to take the blame.

"Maybe we'll see something we recognize on the other side of this hill. Maybe . . . STOP!"

Unit 11: Texas Government Today

Bailey and Ryder slowly stepped away from the tour group. The capitol was cool, but it was crowded. Maybe their parents wouldn't notice. They would stay in sight of their mom and dad, just in case.

As they walked into the rotunda, the boys looked up at the beautiful dome. Their craning necks began to get sore as they picked out the letters: T-E-X-A-S.

But there was something else. Something white. Fluttering, fluttering down.

Bailey reached out his hand, where the paper landed gently. The paper was old and brittle. He gently opened it . . .

BIBLIOGRAPHY

Anderson, Adrian, et al. *Texas and Texans.* New York: Glencoe McGraw-Hill, 2003.

Bailey, Jack. *A Texas Cowboy's Journal.* Norman: University of Oklahoma Press, 2006.

Bevill, James P. *The Paper Republic.* Houston: Bright Sky Press, 2009.

Chrismer, Melanie. *Lone Star Legacy: The Texas Rangers Then and Now*. Gretna: Pelican Publishing Co, 2016.

Connor, Seymore V., et al. *Capitols of Texas.* Waco: Texian Press, 1970.

Cooper, Fred. *Ballads of Texas History*, Frisco: Sing 'n Learn Publications, 2015.

Day, James, et al. *Six Missions of Texas.* Waco: Texian Press, 1965.

Durham, Merle. *The Lone Star State Divided: Texans and the Civil War*. Dallas: Hendrick-Long Publishing Co., 1994.

Feldman, Ruth Tenzer. *The Mexican-American War: Chronicle of America's Wars*. Minneapolis: Lerner Publications Co, 2004.

Foster, Nancy Haston. *Texas Missions: The Alamo and Other Texas Missions to Remember*. Houston: Lone StarBooks, 1995.

Gilbert, Charles E., Jr. *Flags of Texas*. Gretna: Pelican Publishing, 1998.

Haley, James L. *Texas: An Album of History*. Garden City: Doubleday & Company, Inc, 1985.

Holz, Robert K., et al. *Texas and Its History*. Austin: Graphic Ideas, Inc, 1972.

Houston History: Volume 4, Number 2, "San Jacinto," Houston: University of Houston Center For Public History, 2007.

Huffines, Alan C. *The Texas War of Independence 1835-1836*. University Park: Osprey Publishing, 2005.

Jerome, Kate, *Texas: What's So Great About This State*, Mount Pleasant: Arcadia Kids, 2010.

Levy, Janey. *The Missions of Texas.* New York: Rosen Publishing, 2010.

McComb, David G. *Texas: A Modern History.* Austin: University of Texas Press, 1989.

My World of Social Studies. Boston: Pearson, 2016.

Moore, Stephen L. *Eighteen Minutes.* Lanham: Republic of Texas Press, 2004.

Newcomb, W.W. Jr. *The Indians of Texas*. Austin: University of Texas Press, 1990.

Parent, Laurence. *Official Guide to Texas State Parks and Historic Sites*. Austin: University of Texas Press, 2008.

Patent, Dorothy Hinshaw. *The Buffalo and the Indians*. New York: Clarion Books, 2006.

Pickman, Richard. *Anglo-American Colonization of Texas.* New York: Power Kids Press, 2010.

Roden, Phil, et al. *Mini-Q's in Texas History*. Evanston: The DBQ Project, 2010.

Sandell, Cindy. *Texas History Supplemental Text*. Plano: VIS Engerprises, 2004.

Somervill, Barbara A. *Texas*. New York: Scholastic, 20+14.

Sorenson, Richard. *Focus on Texas: History and Geography*. Houston: Hendrick-Long Publishing Co, 1995.

Spearing, Darwin. *Roadside Geology of Texas*. Missoula: Mountain Press Publishing, 1991.

Spradlin, Michael P. *Texas Rangers: Legendary Lawmen*. New York: Walker & Company, 2008.

Stephens, A. Ray. *Texas: A Historical Atlas*. Norman: University of Oklahoma Press, 2010.

"The Texans Are Ready," *The Medallion: World War I Special Edition*, Spring 2017. Austin: Texas Historical Commission.

Warren, Betsy, et al. *The Story of Texas.* Austin: Ranch Gate, 1974.

Warren, Betsy. *Explorers in Early Texas.* Dallas: Hendrick-Long Publishing Co., 1992.

Warren, Betsy. *Let's Remember Indians of Texas.* Dallas: Henderson-Long Publishing Company, 1981.

Warren, Betsy. *Let's Remember When Texas Belonged to Spain*. Dallas: Hendrick-Long Publishing, 1981.

Warren, Betsy. *Texas History Timeline*. Dallas: Hendrick-Long Publishing Company, 1996.

Woodward, Walter M. *Sam Houston: For Texas and the Union*. New York: The Rosen Publishing Group, 2003.

Zappler, George. *Learn About Texas Indians*. Austin: Texas Parks and Wildlife Press, 1996.

Online Sources

The Portal to Texas History: https://texashistory.unt.edu/

Texas State Historical Association: https://www.tshaonline.org/home/

National Archives: https://www.archives.gov/

The Library of Congress: https://www.loc.gov/

Regions - Texas Parks and Wildlife: https://tpwd.texas.gov/kids/about_texas/regions/

Regions - Texas Parks and Wildlife: http://tpwd.texas.gov/

Regions - Texas Almanac: texasalmanac.com

Tigua Indians - http://www.ysletadelsurpueblo.org/

Texas Indians - www.texasindians.com

Plains Indians - http://www.unl.edu/plains/

Texas A&M University - www.tamu.edu

Texas Beyond History - https://www.texasbeyondhistory.net/

Texas State Parks: http://tpwd.texas.gov/state-parks

Prickly Pear Cactus: http://www.texasescapes.com/CFEckhardt/Cowboy-Life-3-prickly-pear-cactus.htm

Explorers: http://ageofex.marinersmuseum.org/index.php?page=theexplorers

COPY WORK EXCERPTS

- *The Writings of Sam Houston*, Volume 5, p. 6. (Excerpt from a letter written to John H. Houston, July 31, 1833.)
- "Allen's Reminiscences of Texas 1838-42" in the **Southwestern Historical Quarterly**, *Texas State Historical Association*, volume 18 (1915), p. 295. Find it here: **https://texashistory.unt.edu/ark:/67531/metapth101064/**
- "The Prison Journal of Stephen F. Austin" *The Quarterly of the Texas State Historical Association* Vol. 2, No. 3 (Jan., 1899), pp. 183-210 . Find it here: **https://www.jstor.org/stable/30242781?seq=1#page_scan_tab_contents**
- Byron, Lord, "The Corsair," 1814.
Find it here: **https://archive.org/stream/corsairtale00byrorich/corsairtale00byrorich_djvu.txt**
- Edward, David B., *The History of Texas*, Cincinnatti: J.A. James & Co., 1836.
- Speech by Major General Gordon Granger, Galveston, June 19th, 1865.
Find it here: **https://www.tsl.texas.gov/ref/abouttx/juneteenth.html**
- Holley, Mary Austin, *Texas,* (originally published 1831), Austin: Texas State Historical Association, 1990.
- Lamar, Mirabeau, *Address to the People of Santa Fe,* June 5, 1841.
Find it here: **http://www.tamu.edu/faculty/ccbn/dewitt/santafeexped.htm**
- Mariager, Dagmar, *The Overland Monthly and Out West Magazine*, Volume 14, Issue 80, August 1889, pp. 190-196. (University of Michigan Library collections)
Find it here: **http://quod.lib.umich.edu/cgi/t/text/text-idx?c=moajrnl&idno=ahj1472.2-14.080**
- Reagan, John H.*,Memoirs With Special References to Secession and the Civil War*, New York and Washington: The Neale Publishing Co, 1906, pp. 290-92. **Find it here: https://archive.org/details/memoirswithspeci00reag**
- Winship, George Park, *The Coronado Expedition: 1540-42*, Washington: The U.S. Bureau of American Ethology, 1896.
Find it here: **https://archive.org/details/coronadoexpediti00winsrich**

Made in the USA
Monee, IL
09 August 2023